WHISKY MISCELLANY

WHISKY MISCELLANY
© Iain Slinn 2004
All rights reserved
Published by Hospitality Scotland Ltd.,
48 Glenburn Drive, Inverness,
IV2 4NE
www.whisky-book.com

Line drawings copyright © by 'Pam 2003'
Sketch maps copyright © by Iain Slinn

ISBN 0-9547360-0-1

A CIP catalogue record for this book is available from the British
Library.

Cover design, layout and typesetting by Stephen Young
LaTouveilhe@mac.com

WHISKY MISCELLANY

Concept and text by

IAIN SLINN

HOSPITALITY SCOTLAND LTD

CONTENTS

This is a book designed for browsing through. Entries are listed alphabetically and cross-referenced throughout, helping to take the reader on a relaxing wander through Iain Slinn's WHISKY MISCELLANY

The Index is comprehensively catalogued to assist the reader searching for technical terms.

The Whisky Distilleries of Scotland

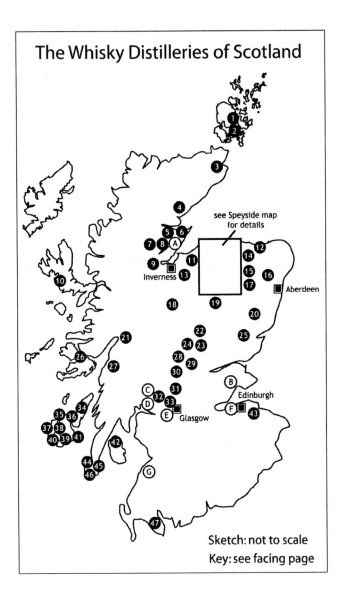

see Speyside map
for details

Inverness

Aberdeen

Edinburgh

Glasgow

Sketch: not to scale
Key: see facing page

MALT DISTILLERIES*

1 Scapa
2 Highland Park
3 Old Pultney
4 Clyneleish
5 Balblair
6 Glenmorangie
7 Dalmore
8 Teaninich
9 Ord
10 Talisker
11 Royal Brackla
12 Macduff
13 Tomatin
14 Knockdhu
15 Glendronach
16 Glengarioch
17 Ardmore
18 Dalwhinnie
19 Royal Lochnagar
20 Fettercairn
21 Ben Nevis
22 Blair Athol
23 Edradour
24 Aberfeldy
25 Glencadam
26 Tobermory
27 Oban
28 Glenturret
29 Tullibardine
30 Deanston
31 Glengoyne
32 Loch Lomond
33 Auchentoshan
34 Isle of Jura
35 Bunnahabhain
36 Caol Ila
37 Bruichladdich
38 Bowmore
39 Lagavulin
40 Laphroaig
41 Ardbeg
42 Isle of Arran
43 Glenkinchie
44 Glen Scotia
45 Springbank
46 Glengyle
47 Bladnoch

GRAIN DISTILLERIES*

A Invergordon
B Cameronbridge
C Loch Lomond
D Port Dundas
E Strathclyde
F North British
G Girvan

*known to be operating

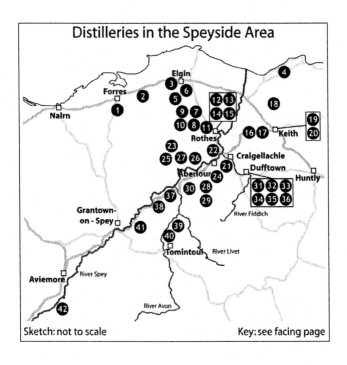

Distilleries in the Speyside Area

Sketch: not to scale

Key: see facing page

MALT DISTILLERIES*

1 Benromach
2 Glenburgie
3 Glen Moray
4 Inchgower
5 Miltonduff
6 Linkwood
7 Longmorn
8 Benriach
9 Glen Lossie
10 Mannochmore
11 Glen Elgin
12 Glen Grant
13 Glen Spey
14 Glenrothes
15 Speyburn
16 Auchroisk
17 Glentauchers
18 Aultmore
19 Strathisla
20 Strathmill
21 Craigellachie

22 The Macallan
23 Cardhu
24 Aberlour
25 Tamdhu
26 Dailuaine
27 Knockando
28 Glenallachie
29 Ben Rinnes
30 Glenfarclas
31 Balvenie
32 Kininvie
33 Glenfiddich
34 Dufftown
35 Glendullan
36 Mortlach
37 Cragganmore
38 Tormore
39 The Glenlivet
40 Tomintoul
41 Balmenach
42 Speyside

*known to be operating

ACKNOWLEDGEMENTS

'Not another book about whisky' was the oft repeated refrain and so it is that I must record my indebtedness to the extraordinarily dedicated personnel at the following distilleries, without whom I would not have progressed:

Beatrice Walker at Aberlour; Stuart Thomson at Ardbeg; Gordon Dey at Aultmore; Derek Sinclair at Balblair; Dennis Malcolm at Balmenach; Isabel Coughlin at Bruichladdich; John Maclellan at Bunnahabhain; Drew Sinclair at Dalmore; Rebecca Richardson at Glenfarclas; David Mair at Glenfiddich; Graham Eunson at Glenmorangie; Ed Dodson at Glen Moray; Ian Mackie at Invergordon; Douglas Davidson at Isle of Arran; Michael Heads and Willie Cochrane at Isle of Jura; Robin Shields at Laphroaig; Kate Wright at Springbank; Douglas Campbell at Tomatin.

The illumination of the industry beyond the distillery confines was revealed to me by the kindness of the following people:

Mike Pruden, Bairds Malt; Miss S. Birnie, Grantown-on-Spey; Colin Scott, Chivas Brothers; to all those 'anonymous' who know who they are (and were) at Customs & Excise; Jacqui Seargeant, Dewars; Derek Dryburgh, Insch; Richard Forsyth, Forsyths; Dr Bill Lumsden and Annie Pugh, Glenmorangie plc; Professor Geoffrey Palmer, Heriot-Watt University; Alex Kraaijeveld; Campbell Evans and Fenella Nicholson, The Scotch Whisky Association; Richard Gordon and Arthur Motley, The Scotch Malt Whisky Society; Stewart Mitchell, The Scottish Environment Protection Agency; Ronnie Grant, Speyside Cooperage; Marcin Miller, Paragraph Publishing.

To the many family members and friends who nodded politely and said 'Oh!' when informed about my current pre-occupation and then produced some very useful 'nuggets'; to 'Pam 2003' for the delightful sketches and to the many individuals who kindly responded to the publicity carried by the local newspapers in the vicinity of Scotland's distilleries –

to all of you, a big 'thanks'. Charles MacLean cannot escape mention: his kind words of encouragement arrived at a most opportune moment. The experience of David P. Webster OBE, in writing and publishing his numerous books on strength sports, was made freely available to me by this indefatigable gentleman.

This book owes a great deal to my editing support team of Mark Whitcombe and Jean Duguid with their eagle eyes and enthusiastic red pens and to Stephen Young's professional skills, gleaned from his days as Editor of The Northern Scot. The latter's kindness and assistance went far beyond the call of duty.

My wife Elaine recovered well from the shock news that 'I'm writing a book' and proved a most useful sounding board and, 'in extremis', chauffeuse.

This book is dedicated to all of the above people and to everyone who has the remotest interest in this fascinating subject.

SOURCES

These have been attributed where the individuals and companies kindly agreed to be associated with the fact. In a number of instances, and for various reasons, others did not wish to appear in print. There are many facts which have common sources across the industry and they therefore remain un-attributable.

The following books provided invaluable factual reference points: *The Malt Whisky Companion*, Michael Jackson, Dorling Kindersley Ltd., London, 1999; *The Making of Scotch Whisky*, Michael S. Moss and John R. Hume; James & James, Edinburgh, 1981; *The Oxford English Dictionary*, Oxford University Press; *Chambers Scots Dictionary*, W. & R. Chambers, Edinburgh, 1975; *The Concise Scots Dictionary*, Aberdeen University Press, 1985; *The Imperial Gazetteer of Scotland*, A. Fullerton & Co., London & Edinburgh circa 1866 and the indispensable *Scotch Whisky Questions and Answers*, The Scotch Whisky Association, Edinburgh, 2002.

The whisky industry continues to be an art and a science. In the course of the author's research it was evident that all involved do not necessarily agree on the facts. This may therefore influence certain material contained within this text. Should you wish to suggest new fascinating facts* please e-mail them to comments@whisky-book.com – or post them to the author at Hospitality Scotland Ltd., 48 Glenburn Drive, Inverness, IV2 4NE.

* In so doing, you are accepting that your suggestion may be used by the author and/or the publisher, in subsequent editions and projects. If so used, you will be acknowledged as the source in subsequent editions and projects. You may prefer not to be quoted as the source, in which case please make your preference clear.

INTRODUCTION

The concept for this book stemmed from a gift that I and many people received in our Christmas Stocking – 'Schott's Original Miscellany'.

Around that time I had become involved in a project where I was looking at information about the whisky industry and I came across some 'fascinating facts' of which I had hitherto been unaware. As a fifty five year old Scot with my cherished 'dram' in the chiffonier, I had started my career witnessing the 'boom' in distillery construction in Banffshire in the early '70's. Now I realised there were 'facts' which I had not fully digested and retained: this despite having visited many distilleries in my day.

Thus, an idea was born.

My research of current publications on whisky suggested that a number were written from the standpoint of the connoisseur – tasting notes etc. – and from the angle of history/folklore. I appreciate that this is something of a generalisation, but I was unable to find a publication which approached the topic from my standpoint. Gavin Smith's excellent work 'A to Z of Whisky', Neil Wilson Publishing Ltd., 1997 comes close but, fortunately, I had developed my own concept before sitting down to read his text.

The 'web' does, of course, offer a source of 'fascinating facts', but as anyone who has tried to peruse this single source is aware, it is damnably inconvenient and certainly not conducive to mulling over a few facts whilst enjoying a dram in comfort at the fireside.

I was particularly concerned to adhere to 'facts', hence my desire to attribute sources and much time was taken in having material vetted. Nevertheless, one of the more interesting facts to emerge was: 'Don't quote me, but…'. This is an industry that cherishes its integrity.

The book is aimed not at the whisky purist, but instead at those who relax at the fireside with their dram and, whilst reflecting upon its contents, might care to peruse some fascinating facts about whisky. For that reason I concentrate upon facts, both serious and of a more light-hearted vein. As Charles MacLean remarked in his kind letter of encouragement, 'You are taking on a potentially huge task, but one which will be great fun, and which you can trim to your own interests'.

Indeed the scope of the task became somewhat daunting as I quickly realised that I could easily be side-tracked. I have therefore adhered to the original concept which was to avoid matters relating to tasting and nosing. I have resisted the urge to relate the plethora of fascinating tales that came to my attention, although some facts could not be allowed to pass unrecorded. Historical material has been kept to a minimum, because this has been more than adequately covered by other writers.

From an historical perspective I was conscious of the fact that I may have been writing at a pivotal time for the ordinary visitor. There can be little doubt that the days of the general public being shown around distilleries by the Distillery Manager or by one of his technical assistants are numbered. Setting aside reasons of utilising manpower most efficiently, the author is of the opinion that the distilleries which are owned by the international conglomerates will increasingly channel the public to those of their distilleries which have Visitor Centres geared to handling the public. The remaining distilleries are likely to face the full weight of 'regulations' as Government departments and the distillers' own insurance companies begin to curtail the movement of the public around distilleries. I sincerely hope that I will be proven wrong, but the portents do not bode well for the future of this traditional hospitality at certain of the smaller distilleries. Some of the smaller distilleries may well find that they can develop their own 'niche' for visitors by introducing more technically interesting tours, for example a half-way house between the current standard 30 – 40 minute 'tour' and the rigorous approach adopted by some of the embryonic 'Whisky Academy Tours'. There is certainly a place for this segment of visitors, who most probably would be quite happy to pay for the privilege

I have avoided the temptation to publish facts which merely served to promote a particular brand, company or distillery, other than those which I considered fascinating. If the reader spots a repetition of sources from one company or another, this is purely down to the fact that their personnel were exceptionally supportive.

Certainly, I can now claim to understand a great deal more about an industry that is integral to the fabric of Scotland. Understandably, the visitor partaking of the average 'distillery tour' can never hope to absorb all the 30 – 40 minutes' knowledge with which they are bombarded. In addition, I hope the reader finds other facts which are rarely mentioned on distillery tours, to be of interest. For those who are stimulated to learn a little bit more about this fascinating industry, I would urge them to seek out the facts: they will not be disappointed.

I set out to compile some 'fascinating facts about whisky'. I leave the reader to decide whether they are as intrigued by the industry as I now am. If not, perhaps 'A Whisky Miscellany' will prompt them to further enquiries.

FROM BARLEY TO BOTTLE

HOW IS IT MADE?

At the risk of offending greatly all who devote their lives to producing whisky, may I state how I like to describe the process of producing a bottle of *single malt*. I fully appreciate that this will rile many, but nevertheless it is broadly what all visitors are told as they prepare to be led off through the labyrinth of a 'distillery tour'.

Take some barley and change it into malted barley*. Grind it and then mix it with hot water. Drain off the water, add some yeast to this liquid and let the concoction ferment.

When the fermentation has ceased, take this 'brew' and distil it. During the distillation process inside these mystical copper stills, the vapours are led off through a thing that cools the vapour. The result is a clear white spirit.

Put this clear white spirit into an oak barrel, store it in a cool place with a constant temperature and be patient – for at least three years. Thereafter, you can probably claim to have made a single malt whisky. If you have kept it in Scotland and abided by the rules and regulations of The Scotch Whisky Act 1988, you will also be able to call your dram 'Scotch'.

With apologies once again to all in the industry for this gross over-simplification and, urging all who wish to learn more, to obtain a copy of the most informative and easily digested publication from The Scotch Whisky Association, 20 Atholl Crescent, Edinburgh, EH3 8HF, entitled: 'Scotch Whisky Questions and Answers'.

* see entry under Malted Barley

A

ABERFELDY DISTILLERY
The excellent '**Trivia Quiz**' at **Dewar's World of Whisky** is the ideal pastime for an inclement day in this area of Perthshire.
Also: Advertising; Bagpipes; Dewarisms; Going, Going....;
Philosopher; Puggie

ABERLOUR DISTILLERY
Exiting the village southward along the Spey Valley, you can easily miss the discreet entrance to this distillery. If you did, you would miss a unique aspect of visiting Aberlour: tasting the **wort** in the mash tuns and tasting the **wash** in the wash backs. The former, which is the liquid derived from steeping the malted barley in hot water, has a very sweet taste; the latter is the fermented wort and it has a very sour taste. It so happens that this most informative of distillery visits also ends with an instructive nosing and tasting of some of the parent company's products, including tasting **new make spirit**.
Also: Sour Beer

ACADEMY
Not quite 'back to school', but for intrepid students of the Islay single malt, you may care to note that Bruichladdich Distillery is now operating a **Whisky Academy**. After a one week residential course at this traditional distillery your 'Curriculum Vitae' may prove of greater interest to prospective employers.

ADAPTABILITY
Whilst the whisky industry has had to change with the times, often taking considerable risks when trying to promote new concepts in marketing, Springbank stands out as a distillery which demonstrates versatility 'in-house'.

Here, no less than three distinct single malt whiskies are made using the same equipment: **Hazelburn** – thrice distilled and with its malt devoid of peat influence; **Longrow** – twice distilled and with its high peaty malt at 45-50 ppm (parts per million); and finally, **Springbank** – two and a half times distilled and with its moderate peaty malt at 15 ppm. In addition, whilst the malt used for the production of Hazelburn is only **air dried** in the traditional kiln, that for the Springbank is dried over the **peat** 'reek' for 6 hours, but the malted barley for Longrow receives a thorough 48 hours drying over the peat smoke, percolating up through the floor of the **kiln house** (source: distillery visit).

Also: Cycle of Production; Glengyle Distillery; Malting Process; Metric or Imperial; Springbank Distillery

ADVERTISING
Tommy Dewar was clearly a man ahead of his time when he observed: 'Keep advertising and advertising will keep you'. In 1898 Dewar's was, in fact, the first to produce an **advertising film** for whisky (source: John Dewar & Sons Ltd).

Also: Laphroaig Distillery

AGE
Life does not necessarily begin at 40 – a statement from Bruichladdich in response to the question 'Is older better?' (source: Bruichladdich Distillery Company Ltd).

Also: All Change; Cloudy

AGED INVENTORY
Those companies undertaking the **blending** of whisky will invariably hold their own stock of different single malts and single grain whisky. The stock is generally purchased direct from specific distilleries as **new make spirit** (the newly made alcohol running off from either the copper **pot still** in the malt distillery or the **column still** in the grain distillery). This new **distillate** will be matured in warehouses in casks of different sizes (barrels; hogsheads; butts) that have previously held

[Bold text within paragraphs refers to sub-headings in the Index]

Sherry, Bourbon or Scotch whisky. Age, condition and volumes will be carefully monitored (and recorded in the Aged Inventory) so that when the **Blender** requires to use a specific malt or grain whisky from his 'recipe book' and make a particular blend, he knows that he has access to sufficient stock to ensure the production flow for the bottling line (source: Colin Scott. Master Blender, Chivas Brothers).

Also: Master Blender; Players and Managers

AGE (of drinker)

The Scotch Malt Whisky Society has observed that there is a common connection between the older, gentleman drinker and 'big **sherried whiskies**' (source: Arthur Motley, The Scotch Malt Whisky Society).

AGE (on a label)

By law this refers to the **youngest whisky** used in the blend, no matter how small the amount. It is never an average. (source: The Scotch Whisky Association).

ALCOHOL BY VOLUME

Most whisky on sale in Britain has a strength of 40 per cent alcohol by volume (abv). Whisky for export generally has an abv of 43 per cent. This contrasts with the strength of the product when it is placed in casks for maturing. Single malt whisky* is generally filled into the casks at 63.5 per cent. In each instance the 'new make spirit' has been reduced in strength by the addition of water to its distilled alcoholic strength. As laid down in the **Scotch Whisky Act of 1988**, the latter is not permitted to exceed 94.8 per cent. This ensures that the distillate has an aroma and taste derived from the raw materials used in its production (source: The Scotch Whisky Association: 'Scotch Whisky Questions & Answers')

Also: Scotch Whisky Act 1988

* Single grain whisky (for example Invergordon) is generally filled into casks at 71 per cent alcohol by volume.

ALL CHANGE
With a view to re-establishing itself in the market place, **Bruichladdich** is now bottled at a higher strength; without chill filtration or colouring; in a new bottle design and with new labelling (source: Bruichladdich Distillery Company Ltd).

AMINO ACIDS
Contained within the malted barley, amino acids are known to play a central role in distilling because they support yeast growth. This is essential for the production of **alcohol**. Amino acids are also converted into **flavour compounds** during the **kilning process** and by the **yeast** during the later fermentation stage (source: G.H. Palmer, Professor of Cereal Science, Heriot Watt University; 'A Wee Dram of Whisky' in Liquid Foods International; January, 1999).

Also: Cosmetics

ANGELS' SHARE *
The author had the good fortune to win a crate of The Balvenie in the early 1980s. Setting aside a bottle over-night on the dining room table to give as a present to 'the old man', imagine the shock next morning to discover that the 'angels' had entered the house during the night. The bottle, which had not moved from its horizontal position on the tablecloth and with seal still intact, had lost half its contents. This extraordinary phenomenon was reported to Balvenie Distillery, the bottle returned intact and forensic tests over some three months finally elicited the response from Balvenie: 'An inexplicable set of circumstances!'

Also: Laying Down; Win Some, Lose Some

* This is the colloquial term given to the quantity of whisky lost to evaporation from the casks during maturation in the warehouse.

ANIMAL FEED
The waste material from the mash tuns (termed **draff**) from certain distilleries is sent for processing to a specialist **Dark**

[Bold text within paragraphs refers to sub-headings in the Index]

Grains Plant – some distilleries continue to have this plant on site – where it is mixed with the **Burnt Ale** (the waste from the first distillation). The liquid is then squeezed out to leave a dark fibrous substance. This is made into pellets and sold to farmers, whereby their cattle are able to enjoy their own 'dram'!

Also: Burnt Ale; Dark Grains; Environmentally Friendly

ANNIVERSARY

Every year at 11.00am on the 11th day of the 11th month, a ceremony is held at **Yamazaki Distillery** in Japan (built in 1923 by Shinjiro Torii, founder of Suntory Ltd). The occasion commemorates and celebrates the day when 'the first Japanese whisky was born'. It also acts as a timely reminder to all distillery staff to improve quality and their skills (source: Masami Onishi, in The Scotch Malt Whisky Society Newsletter, Winter 2003).

Also: Japan

ANOSMIA

Those suffering from this ailment need not apply for the position of Blender.

Also: Master Blender

ANSWER

Check the Index for 'Answer'.

ANTIDOTE

A lady in Angus was rushed to hospital after accidentally drinking **anti-freeze** and was given **alcohol** as an antidote. Ninewells Hospital in Dundee told her the only cure was to drink alcohol, and plenty of it. She opted for whisky and was ordered to drink two cupfuls immediately.

The hospital authorities had pointed out that consuming anti-freeze is potentially serious. Someone who takes only 100mls of anti-freeze could die. Throughout the night, nursing staff provided her with a measure of whisky every hour while monitoring the level of anti-freeze in her blood. The following day, the dosage was reduced to a 'nip' and by afternoon she was allowed to stagger home.

Also: Measles

ANTI – SMOKING
In the late 1950s a blind Italian musician, Valentino Zagatti of Lugo di Ravena decided to spend his cigarette money more wisely. He opted to collect whisky. The upshot is that his house is now home to some 4,000 bottles, of which over half are malts (source: J. & G. Grant's Autumn Review, 2000).

ARK ROYAL
All 20,000 tonnes of the Royal Navy's aircraft carrier anchored off Ardbeg Distillery in mid June 2003 and a lucky 50 of her crew nipped ashore as part of a useful exercise. The visit was reciprocated with ten of the distillery staff, in need of similar exercise, enjoying the hospitality of the ship's captain in the officers' mess.

ARRAN DISTILLERY
Opened in 1995 this was the first of the 'new' distilleries since the boom of the mid-seventies.

Also: Golden Eagles; Ducks

ARTISTS
Glenfiddich Distillery has an 'Artists in Residence' programme, whereby international artists are invited to live and work in and around the distillery for 2 – 3 months each summer. A gallery of exhibits complements the work of the Artists in Residence (source: Wm Grant & Sons).

ASSAY
Some in the whisky industry are now seeking to capitalise on this symbol of integrity, more commonly associated with the hallmarking of precious metals such as gold and silver. Diageo

[Bold text within paragraphs refers to sub-headings in the Index]

has given its highly successful Classic Malts a 'make-over' to create 'The Distillers Edition'. To quote from the label on the bottle(s): 'Each special limited edition is hallmarked as a symbol of rarity and superior quality'. The bottle carries the assay mark for: the specific distillery; the year the distillery was established; the wood-type for the second maturation and finally the monogram for each Master Distiller. Each 'Distillers Edition' is marketed as 'double matured' and in the case of Talisker, for example, the cask wood used in the second maturation is specified as 'Jerez Amorozo'.

Also: Diageo

AUCHROISK DISTILLERY

Built in the **boom years** of 1973 – '74 this distillery markets its single malt under the title of **The Singleton** (slightly easier for customers to pronounce).

Also: Bar One

AULTMORE DISTILLERY

From 1898 until 1969, the principal source of power used to drive all working plant and machinery at this distillery was a 10hp **Abernethy Steam Engine** built by the **Ferryhill Foundry** in Aberdeen. Although no longer in working order, this engineering stalwart takes pride of place inside the distillery (source: John Dewar & Sons Ltd).

Also: Computers; Environmentally Friendly

B

BAGPIPES

The pulling power of the 'pipes was ably demonstrated by **Tommy Dewar** at the 1886 Brewers' Show, when not only did he make a dramatic entrance to the Show, but continued to deafen his audience despite the organiser's instructions to desist. The ensuing **publicity** was a godsend for the dynamic brothers Tommy and John Dewar, as they tried to penetrate the market in England (source: John Dewar & Sons Ltd)

Also: Clann An Drumma

BALANCING THE BOOKS

Do you have problems with your household budget? Spare a thought for the Distillery Manager. He is legally responsible for safeguarding the (potential) revenue value of the spirits he produces and stores on his property, all of which is contained within the **duty suspended system**. Cutting through the **Customs & Excise** legislation, this boils down to 'the trader' having to account for all materials used; all spirits produced; all receipts and deliveries; all of the numerous operations – for example, filling into casks, blending, and so forth; all storage; all stock control and all security. Now, whilst much of this might arguably be done automatically by good management, the rub is that a failure to balance the books monthly can result in draconian **financial penalties.**

Also: Every Last Drop Counts; Reciprocals; Record Keeping; Tax

BALBLAIR DISTILLERY

There can be few more charming distillery settings than that of Balblair. Built to the design of **Charles Doig** – he of numerous distillery creations – and complete with its 'pagoda-style' kiln roof dominating the small courtyard, this is one of those few

[Bold text within paragraphs refers to sub-headings in the Index]

remaining distilleries which continue to offer **tours by appointment only**. Don't miss the classic **dunnage warehouses**, the fire alarm bell and also some arresting artist's impressions of distillery life.

Also: 'Pagoda'; Spile The Knot

BALL AND STRING

At Tomatin, the art of **'sounding'** the wash stills to establish how high up in the neck the liquid is rising during the distillation process is by the old traditional method of ball and string. Nearly all distilleries have now introduced the modern **sight glass** window in the neck of the still to monitor froth levels (source: distillery visit).

Author's Note: a **sight glass** is only required in the Wash Still and not in the **Low Wines and Feints Still** because there is no longer any yeast left in the Low Wines (source: Dallas Dhu)

BALLINDALLOCH

In the early 1960s, the twice weekly whisky freight trains started from Craigellachie and collected wagons from Aberlour, Carron, Dailuaine, Knockando and Ballindalloch, heading south via Aviemore to the warehouses and bottling plants in the Central Belt and beyond.

Ballindalloch Station was on an incline and by the time the train reached here, it had collected so many wagons of whisky that it was impossible to leave on the onward journey from a standing start. Consequently, about half a mile before reaching the station the engine was uncoupled from the wagons and steamed up to Ballindalloch to collect the local consignment before reversing back down the line to pick up the train again. This allowed the driver to take a good run at the slope and with a big load, the impetus was just enough to carry him through Ballindalloch Station and on his way (source: Bill Murray, Fair Isle and formerly employed at Ballindalloch Station).

Also: Dramming; Railway Drams; Transport

BALVENIE DISTILLERY

Nowhere else will you find a distillery that still grows its own barley, still malts in its own traditional **floor maltings** and still employs coopers to tend the casks and a coppersmith to maintain the stills. The traditional maltings at Balvenie Distillery are used only for making 'The Balvenie' (source: Balvenie Distillery).

Also: Angels' Share

BANK OF SCOTLAND

Feel the quality. Next time a current Bank of Scotland £10 sterling note passes through your hands, pause to reflect that you are handling three of the copper stills from The Macallan Distillery (source: HBOS Group Archives, Edinburgh, 2003).

Also: Edrington Group Ltd

BARLEY

If the farmer's crop is not up to standard – for example, the harvest of 2002 produced a relatively poor crop – the production of whisky may suffer. With poor quality barley, the ensuing critical statistic of **alcohol yield per tonne of malted barley** will drop – it fell by some 3% as a result of the 2002 harvest – but energy, labour and other fixed production costs cannot be reduced to compensate. The net effect is to impinge upon profitability. A low-yielding barley will of course fetch a lower price when sold to the Maltings and in turn this is reflected in the price paid by the distillery when they purchase the malted barley from the Maltings. The corollary is that poor harvests create a shortage of quality malt and demand drives up prices for the scarce, prime malted barley. All Maltings will give a predicted alcohol yield per tonne of malted barley which they offer for sale.

To try to anticipate poor harvests, the Maltings will check the progression of the farmers' crops from May onwards. The farmers have to meet independently verified production and storage standards as laid down by **Scottish Quality Cereals**. In

[Bold text within paragraphs refers to sub-headings in the Index]

extreme seasons, it is not unknown for the barley to be imported but a number of the distillery companies find the additional cost and potential adverse publicity counter-productive.

Some distillers, Maltings and farmers work so closely together to try to achieve the required standards that the barley can be traced back to the original field. Bairds Malt with its subsidiary company **Scotgrain Agriculture Ltd** of Forfar is a case in point. With large trial sites located in some of Scotland's prime barley growing areas, Scotgrain is in a strong position to customise production for its distillery clients.

Also: Maltings; Raw Material Costs; Tonnes and Litres

BARLEY – 'AS HARD AS HENDERSON'S'

This expression from the Buchan area of North East Scotland, could easily be applied to the grains of barley. The **abrasive quality** of the barley is borne out by old distillery hands who would talk about razor sharp edges to moving metal parts which came into regular contact with the flow of barley through the mill. Scott Hardie of Inverness showed the author a section of the wooden barley chute from **Ord Distillery** (where his grandfather worked) – the surface had very distinct ripple flow-lines the length of the surface (as if on a dried up river bed) clearly indicating the direction of flow of the barley.

BAR MALTS

The average number of malt whiskies stocked in Scottish bars is seven and in English pubs, two (source: Charles MacLean in The Scotch Malt Whisky Society Newsletter summer 2001)

BAR ONE

The licensed premises of The **Byron Darnton Tavern** on the Island of **Sanda** (located off the Kintyre Peninsula) may in future be tempted to stock **The Singleton**. The pub has one regular local, ensuring that the staff is always gainfully employed. The proprietor doubles as both!

Also: Auchroisk Distillery

BARRELS

By definition, Scotch Whisky can only be matured in oak **casks** (the generic term used in the industry is 'cask' in order not to be confused with the quite specific 'American Barrel'). The majority of oak casks are obtained from the American Bourbon manufacturers because, under the laws of the USA, a bourbon barrel can only be used once. The Macallan is an exception to this rule, using casks made from the oak of **Galicia's forests**, in which sherry is stored, prior to the casks being exported to Speyside. Nearly all imported casks arrive in Scotland as bundles of staves, the original bourbon barrels having been broken down for efficiency of transport. Kenneth Kilby in his book 'The Cooper and His Trade' (Linden Publishing 1989) explains that these '**shooks**' would be individually numbered in order that they could be re-assembled in exactly the same sequence. By contrast, casks imported by distillers who value top quality wood (for example The Macallan and Glenmorangie plc) are shipped intact or '**standing**' and with bungs in place, in order to retain the maximum amount of the essential qualities from the sherry and bourbon maturation process in Spain and The United States, respectively (source: distillery visits).

Also: Ozark Mountains

BARS

Tokyo has some 10,000 'Whisky Bars'. One such, 'Nemo', stocks over 4,500 bottles of whisky.

BLACK BARREL

This single grain whisky is produced by Wm Grant & Sons' grain distillery at **Girvan**. It is matured in charred – 'torched' – barrels.

Also: Charring; Distillation Times 2.5

BLACK BOTTLE

A blended whisky which incorporates all of the seven **Islay Malts** (source: The Islay and Jura Whisky Trail Leaflet).

[Bold text within paragraphs refers to sub-headings in the Index]

BLADNOCH DISTILLERY

Tucked away in the depths of South West Scotland, **Raymond Armstrong** purchased this mothballed distillery from the uninterested United Distillers (now part of Diageo) and re-opened it for the benefit of visitors in the year 2000. Production is limited to approximately 100,000 litres per annum and sales are predominantly through the Visitor Centre.

BLENDED SCOTCH WHISKY

A 'blend' will consist of anything from 15 – 50 different single whiskies (malt and grain whiskies) combined in the proportions of a formula that is the secret of the blending company concerned. Blended whiskies account for 95 per cent of all **Scotch Whisky*** sold in world markets (source: The Scotch Whisky Association).

Also: EU; Exports; Seconds Away

* A typical blended Scotch Whisky is made up of 60 – 65 per cent grain whisky. TESCO own brand Scotch Whisky Reserve is a blend of 30 per cent malt and 70 per cent grain whisky.

BLENDER'S AIMS

These include: to produce a whisky of a definite and recognisable character; to achieve consistency so that customers will enjoy the same standard that they have come to expect, and to decide when the different single whiskies are ready to be used in the particular blend (source: The Scotch Whisky Association, 2003)

Also: Impact; Marrying

BLENDER'S NOSE

It is possible for experienced Blenders to differentiate between well-known established brands of Scotch Whisky by **smell** alone. At the most, a Blender will moisten their hands with a little of the spirit, but usually it is enough to smell the whisky in a 'nosing' glass (source: The Scotch Whisky Association).

Also: Anosmia; Smell and Taste

BLENDING

'A science influenced by the art of experience and good judgement', is how the author summarised his introduction to blending, courtesy of Colin Scott, Master Blender, Chivas Brothers. Revealing no secrets, the writer was privileged to see how the subtle variations in matured single malts and single grains can influence the 'recipe'. Indeed, the analogy with the kitchen cook is a very apt one: alter certain ingredients and the end product changes – this applies to new products. But to maintain **consistency** of an established product, where over the years whiskies may or may not be available, the art of blending will ensure that although the number of whiskies may change, the final product does not. Blending requires rigorous **attention to detail** and meticulous record keeping, if all the various experiments (for new blends) and continuous production of existing blends, is not to be put at risk.

Also: New Blends; Players and Managers; Popularity

BLENDING TROUGH

Wm Grant & Sons (of Glenfiddich fame) pioneered Scotland's first-ever automatic blending trough at their **Girvan** (grain) distillery, a process that led to greater speed and efficiency when handling the cumbersome casks (source: The Pioneering Spirit, 1995). Reminding one for all the world of a **sheep dip** on a Highland farm, this remarkably simple arrangement permits the contents of a dozen Hogsheads (as in the one at **Tomatin**) to be emptied easily into the trough. The mixture is then pumped up into the **blending tank** where it is suitably stirred and then shipped out for further processing, according to its intended end use (source: distillery visit).

Also: Supermarket Influence

BLENDS – A MARKETING DREAM

The science and art of blending allow the industry to maintain the quality of established whisky brands, while providing the opportunity of developing **new brands** to meet the demands of

[Bold text within paragraphs refers to sub-headings in the Index]

the consumer (source: G.H. Palmer, Professor of Cereal Science, Heriot Watt University; 'A Wee Dram of Whisky' in Liquid Foods International; January, 1999).

Also: Forecasting Demand

BLENDS, BLENDS, BLENDS

In the absence of a comprehensive list, here is a '**blenders' dozen**' of blended Scotch: Abbot's Choice; Chequers; John Barr; King's Ransom; Lismore; Old Court; Old Orkney; Old Parr; Putachieside; Rob Roy; Robbie Burns; Royal Heritage; Té Bheag nan Eilean.

Also: Vanishing Distilleries

BOTTLED BY

The **Scotch Malt Whisky Society's whisky** is bottled at Glenmorangie's bottling plant in Broxburn. Prior to this, the bottling was undertaken by **Drambuie** in Kirkliston (source: The Scotch Malt Whisky Society).

BOTTLES

The distinctive '**three-sided-shape**' of the Glenfiddich and Grant's bottle, was pioneered by Wm Grant & Sons in 1957 (source: The Pioneering Spirit, 1995).

Also: Plastic

BOTTLES (BOUNCING)

The author has been assured by the staff on the bottling line at

Bruichladdich Distillery, that, provided their distinctive bottles land correctly on the concrete floor, they do not break (source: distillery visit).

Also: Testing

BOTTLING LINES
Springbank, Glenfiddich and Bruichladdich distilleries are the only distilleries to have bottling lines on site.

BOURBON WHISKEY
The **United States' Regulations** provide:

(i) that Bourbon Whiskey must be produced from a mash of not less than 51 per cent corn grain;

(ii) that the word 'Bourbon' shall not be used to describe any whiskey or whiskey-based distilled spirits not produced in the United States. (source: The Scotch Whisky Association).

Also: Rye Whiskey

BOWMORE
And another sound reason for visiting this distillery – the delightful little town of the same name (on the island of Islay) has Scotland's only **round church**. Designed by a French architect in the mid 18th century, it is reputed that he gave it a rounded shape in order that there would be no corners in which the Devil might hide.

Also: Fly Fishing; Swimming Pool; Tides; Vice-consul

BRANCHING OUT
The Scotch Malt Whisky Society has branches in the United States, the Netherlands, France, Italy, Switzerland, Austria and Japan (source: The Scotch Malt Whisky Society).

BRAND PROTECTION
The industry is built on 'brands' and **image**. Understandably, most distillers will do everything possible to guard against jeopardising this status and will not hesitate to

prosecute any who infringe their Trademark. Given that a distillery will also sell some of its '**new make spirit**' for blending purposes – to companies out-with its direct control – this can pose certain problems. The simplest way around this is for the distillery to mix some of its product with a little of another distillery and give the resultant 'mix' a distinctive and separate name. Alternatively, they can sell to trusted customers, who undertake to label their bottles with vague descriptions of locality of origin – as in the case of sales to The Scotch Malt Whisky Society, supermarkets and other bulk buyers.

Also: Buy The Cask

BRANDS

More than 2,500 brands of Scotch Whisky are sold all over the world, of which as many as 200 are available in the **home market**. Many brands are sold only locally, or to private clubs and individuals (source: The Scotch Whisky Association).

Also: VAT 69

BRUICHLADDICH DISTILLERY

This distillery uses the original 1881 **Victorian machinery** – now expertly restored to full working order (source: distillery visit).

Also: 'Enfants Terribles'; Equity; Spring Water

BUBBING

This, the process of mixing yeast and **wort** to promote fermentation, requires the express written permission of HM Customs and Excise (source: Notice 39, 2002 clause 6.7).

BULK SHIPMENTS

When whisky is exported in bulk to overseas markets, glass lined, stainless steel tanks or traditional casks will be used for its **transportation** (source: The Scotch Whisky Association).

BUNGS
The cooper who knows his trade will prefer to use bungs made from **American Poplar** instead of oak. The former are more malleable.

BUNNAHABHAIN DISTILLERY
If you stick to the 'popular' distilleries of Islay, you will unquestionably miss one of the great surprises of this island. Tucked away at the end of the road, the impression gained as you approach, is of a tiny distillery nestling in the corner of the bay. Nothing quite prepares you for the extensive distillery complex which is to be found along much of the foreshore. With the largest mash tun on the island, Bunnahabhain and its eleven staff are capable of producing 2.2 million litres of alcohol per annum (production in 2003 was running at 50 per cent capacity). Only recently acquired by CL World Brands from The Edrington Group, this is a distillery impatient to re-establish itself in the market place (source: distillery visit).

Also: Ownership

BURNS
In his capacity as an Exciseman, Robert Burns was stationed for a time in Campbeltown and it was allegedly here, that he met his 'Sweet Highland Mary' (source: Springbank Distillery).

BURNT ALE
One of the founders of Laphroaig Distillery – Donald Johnston – died in 1847 two days after falling into a 'Burnt Ale' vat. Also known as **pot ale** or **spent wash**, this is the waste liquid left in the **Wash Still** after the first distillation. Properly sprayed over the fields, this liquid has been recognised by certain farmers as a very beneficial fertiliser. It is not unusual for farmers local to their distillery to agree contracts with the distillery to uplift the Burnt Ale. Some distilleries such as Aberlour, reduce the pot ale by evaporation to produce 'Pot Ale

[Bold text within paragraphs refers to sub-headings in the Index]

Syrup'. This is then sold through agents to farmers, as a concentrated supplement feed for cattle, or sent to the Dark Grains 'factory' where it is added to the **draff** (the solid waste from the Mash Tun) and finally made into pellets for animal feed.

Author's note: the industry has had its fair share of unfortunate incidents over the years and whilst some may have become embellished with the passing of time, the employee who disappeared only to be traced by his **false teeth** sets the tone for what could befall those who fell into certain containers.

Also: Dark Grains; Laphroaig Distillery

BUY THE CASK

For readers who fear being cut off from their favourite dram and who believe in **laying down** a bottle or two for a rainy day, you will be pleased to know that there is one top quality distillery still prepared to sell you a cask: Bruichladdich. With producers and blenders now much more reluctant to sell by the cask (there is justifiable fear that brand **image** may be compromised) it is gratifying to find this innovative distillery thinking of the customer's needs as well as their own. Drawbacks? – possibly two: you have to wait for the cask to mature in their warehouse on Islay and you will be looking at a minimum of 200 litres – less the Angel's Share (approximately 15 – 20 per cent loss over 10 years).

Also: Brand Protection

C

CAMPBELTOWN

The Imperial Gazetteer of Scotland published by A. Fullerton & Co., states that in the mid 19th century this thriving town had no fewer than 25 distilleries and that 60 persons were employed in the 'Excise establishment'.

Also: Fog; Shipping

CAOL ILA DISTILLERY

Stand beside the copper stills at this distillery and enjoy an unsurpassed vista across the Sound of Islay to the hills of Jura.

CAPACITIES

A **butt** holds 500 litres; a **hogshead** holds 250 – 305 litres; an **American (bourbon) barrel** 173 – 191 litres and a **bottle** 70cl (source: The Scotch Whisky Association).

Also: Puncheon

CARBON DIOXIDE

Some grain whisky distilleries recover this gas which is produced during the fermentation stage. As The Scotch Whisky Association points out, this by-product has several applications in industry and also in the production of soft drinks. However the malt whisky distilleries produce insufficient amounts to make re-processing economic and the gas is simply pumped into the atmosphere.

CHALK

An elderly Cooper had a habit of eating the chalk he used for recording the cask contents during filling operations. His usual comment each morning was 'I wish I was dead'. An hour later and a sample jar of over-proof grain spirit

[Bold text within paragraphs refers to sub-headings in the Index]

consumed, life was worth living again – thanks to the anti-acid chalk treatment that he was taking to ward off the deleterious effects of his daily liquid refreshment (source: Exciseman Anonymous).

CHANGING FORTUNES

If any evidence of the change in circumstances is needed since the last peak of Scotch Whisky production in the early 1970s, it is the instance of one distillery which was supplying **new-make-spirit** to one of the larger distilling groups. This particular distillery has seen its sales to that specific customer drop by some 500 per cent during the intervening 30 years. Demand has dropped due to changes in drinking tastes and habits (not least from the impact of 'clear spirits') and so the original customer is able to obtain sufficient new-make-spirit from its own distilleries.

Figures produced in The Scotch Whisky Association's 'Statistical Report 2002' (pages 4 and 5) demonstrate how the annual total of Scotch Whisky released for current **UK consumption** has fallen by approximately 37 per cent from its previous peak at the end of the 1970s. Fortunately for the industry, **exports** of Scotch Whisky over the same period have continued to expand, reaching a peak in 2001. Nevertheless, combining the two statistics suggests that there has been a slight overall fall in demand across the period 1979 – 2001.

Also: Forecasting Demand; Foresight

CHARCOAL

Some years ago at Glen Grant Distillery, it was the practice to inject high grade flake charcoal with water into every **spirit still charge**. This proved highly satisfactory in speeding the time it took for the spirit to start running clear in the Spirit Safe (source: Dennis Malcolm, formerly at Glen Grant and now at Balmenach Distillery).

Also: Gardens; Glen Grant Distillery

[Bold text within paragraphs refers to sub-headings in the Index]

CHARRING

To obtain the necessary curves in the staves that make up a cask, the traditional craftsmen applied heat to the inside surface and **toasted** the wood. Nowadays, a **cooperage** will use steam to assist in the shaping of the staves.

Charring – which is quite a different process – perhaps evolved from someone 'over-doing the toast' and not revealing their mistake. The subsequent cask may have been found to have produced an even better whisky. The inner surfaces of the staves in a charred cask are very rough, compared to those of a toasted cask, the objective being to create a coating of charcoal. Scientists would point out – as in the revealing paper by G.H. Palmer, Professor of Cereal Science, Heriot Watt University; 'A Wee Dram of Whisky' in Liquid Foods International; January, 1999) – that 'Charring the casks produces: **carbon**, which helps mellow the whisky; **hydrolysable tannins** which promote oxidative reactions such as **ester formation** from acids; lignin flavour compounds such as **vanillins**, which produce vanilla aromas; simple sugars which are responsible for a slight sweetness, whilst malty flavours come from the release of **furfural**, 2-methyl furfural and maltol, due to **pentosan** degradation'.

Also: Oak; Pompeying; Staves

CHEMICAL WEAPONS

Thanks to Bruichladdich and the United States' **Defence Threat Reduction Agency** we now know that in making whisky it is just a short step away from modifying the manufacturing method so that one could be making chemical weapons. This extraordinary revelation (national Press reports September, 2003) came to the attention of the management at Bruichladdich, when one of their recently installed webcams developed a fault. A thoughtful follower of **The Laddie** had dropped them an e-mail asking that it be fixed, just as soon as possible, please. The malt enthusiast? – none other than the dutiful Secret Service Agents of the world's mightiest military

[Bold text within paragraphs refers to sub-headings in the Index]

machine: the United States' Department of Defence Threat Reduction. One can only imagine that the Bourbon industry has at last got word of the serious threat posed by the 'Enfants Terribles' of Islay and are determined to stay one step ahead of the game.

Also: 'Enfants Terribles'

CLANN AN DRUMMA

Whisky promotion takes many forms, but a one year promotional contract sees this five man drum ensemble and piper promoting Ardbeg's interests around the world. The local Islay newspaper 'Ileach' (14th June, 2003) described the band 'Hammering away on these ethnic drums, like demented **Picts** and while the lone piper fights for survival, the rumble hits you in the pit of your stomach'.

Also: Bagpipes

CLASSIC MALTS

Significant breakthroughs in **marketing** will always be debateable, not least because it takes time for specific actions to demonstrate that this is what they have turned out to be. Nevertheless, ranking alongside Wm. Grant and Sons' phenomenal marketing push of the single malt Glenfiddich, has to be The Classic Malts launched by United Distillers. In one stroke six hitherto relatively unknown single malts were thrust into the public domain – **Cragganmore; Dalwhinnie; Glenkinchie; Lagavulin; Oban** and **Talisker.** This marketing concept placed single malts (in general) on an altogether higher plane of publicity and served to cement the increasing popularity of single malts world-wide.

Also: Milestones; Three Sheets In The Wind

CLEANING ROUTINE

Distilleries pride themselves on their cleanliness – some more than others. The author has been shown around some establishments where you could 'eat off the floor'. Glenfarclas is no exception. Here, the author could not help feeling sorry for the man who weekly cleans by hand the inside of the **largest mash tun on Speyside** with wire wool, and twice a week if the distillery is at full production!

Also: Keep Fit: Stay Happy

CLIMATE CHANGE LEVY

In the 1970's the rocketing costs of **energy** caused the whisky industry (and many other industries) to cut out the wasteful use of energy. Today other forces are at work, pressurising energy users to economise with the use of fuel. Distillery Managers are finding The Climate Change Levy a useful means to increase the **efficiency of production**, because company accountants can clearly understand the benefit of alterations which allow the company to achieve its 'target'. The result can be a rebate of up to 80% of the levy. At the time of writing, the responsible Government department (DEFRA) lists all Scotland's grain distilleries and 64% of Scotland's malt distilleries as being covered by a **Climate Change Agreement**.

Also: Milestones

CLOUDY

This is a natural occurrence for non-chill-filtered whisky (for example, Bruichladdich's new bottlings since September, 2001). Such whiskies will become less clear over time as the natural proteins and oils marry following the addition of water. **Chill-filtration** would prevent this, but at the expense of the flavour (source: Bruichladdich Distillery Company Ltd).

CLV

For those readers of a certain age and perception, the letters on the front and back of the lorry, stand for 'Crown Lock Vehicle'. In other words, with the seals intact, the vehicle in question is/was likely to be carrying goods for which no duty had been paid.

[Bold text within paragraphs refers to sub-headings in the Index]

COALS TO NEWCASTLE
The quality of many of the single malts produced in **Japan** is so high that some are being exported to Scotland, where discerning drinkers have been known to compare them to Speyside malts.

COASTAL EFFLUENT
Distilleries on the coastline sometimes dispose of their effluent via a long pipeline leading out into the sea. This saves the cost of transporting the effluent elsewhere for treatment. Consent for the pipeline is issued by the **Scottish Environment Protection Agency** (SEPA). For a discharge to coastal waters, a model will have to be built to demonstrate that the effluent is mixing satisfactorily with the sea water, and that any environmental quality standards are not going to be breached (source: adapted from correspondence received by the author from SEPA).
Also: Effluent; Waste Treatment

COFFEY STILL
Patented in 1830 by an Irishman of that name, this still is used only in grain distilleries and it produces a lighter spirit than a **pot still** (used in malt distilleries). It does this faster, in greater volumes, and at a lower cost than the pot still. This still came into widespread use in the 1860's and its lighter spirit, blended with the heavier, oilier, peatier and younger malt whiskies (which hitherto were the province of Scotland) served to launch blended Scotch Whisky firstly into England and then around the world. To quote from John Dewar & Sons' 'World of Whisky Visitor Guide', the Coffey Still 'changed the world of whisky forever'.
Also: Grain Distilleries

COLLAPSING STILLS
At most distilleries the copper stills are fitted nowadays with an **'Air Cran Valve'** to release the pressure when the still is

emptied. Failure to do so was, in the past, a prime cause for the sides of the still collapsing inwards. A foolproof method is introduced whereby, the lever to operate the valve, is the same lever required to empty and to fill the still – as seen for example, at **Balmenach** and **Bunnahabhain**.

COLLECTORS
Giuseppe Begnoni keeps the world's largest collection of whisky in his Italian warehouse. The contents include some 15,000 different bottles, with 'swops' and other trading stock running to perhaps 50,000 bottles (source: Charles MacLean in The Scotch Malt Whisky Society Newsletter winter 2002).

COLOUR
A number of blenders add a small amount of flavourless colouring caramel to give the desired uniformity in colour.
Also: White Whisky

COLOUR CODING
Next time you are inside a warehouse and you see the proliferation of different coloured casks, you will be told that various companies use different colours to keep track of how often the cask has been used. A simpler method favoured by 'old hands' – such as at **Balmenach** – is to punch the requisite number of holes on the top rim of the exposed barrel.
Also: Warehousing

COMAH
These environmental regulations, enforced jointly by **The Scottish Environment Protection Agency (SEPA)** and **The Health & Safety Executive (HSE)** are currently inducing a 'coma' effect upon a number of distillery managers. The **Control of Major Accidents and Hazards (COMAH)** seeks to regulate against the worst effects stemming from spillage and fires. 'Under these regulations, sites with a certain volume of spirit must carry out a detailed assessment of the risks

[Bold text within paragraphs refers to sub-headings in the Index]

associated with the storage of this flammable material, taking into consideration harm to human health and the environment. Distillers must take the appropriate safety measures to ensure that all steps have been taken to stop or nullify the potential for spillages or accidents, where harm to health or the environment due to an incident such as fire, for example, can occur. The assessments that they carry out require to be inspected and approved by **SEPA** and/or **HSE** and if they are found to be insufficient then prosecution may follow' (quoted from correspondence received by the author from SEPA). The casual visitor encounters the immediate consequence of this new rigour as he/she stumbles over the raised '**bunds**' (10 -15 cm) that now crop up all over the place in distilleries.

Also: Environmentally Friendly

COMMODITY TRADING

There is no organised 'Whisky Exchange' such as exists for other commodities, nor is there any official published list of buying and selling prices for whisky of different types and ages (source: The Scotch Whisky Association).

Also: Reciprocals

COMMUNITIES

It is only by speaking to some retired distillery personnel (and in the case of the author, having been privileged to have visited many distillery communities in the course of his work as a young Planning Officer in Banffshire in the early 1970s) that one realises just how close-knit these small collections of people were. This also included the **Excise Officer**, who was invariably seen as a key member of the community. It was he who policed the un-written rule which bound the community together: 'Nobody ever sold anything'. As with all local communities, those at the distilleries were not without their 'characters'. Occasionally, there might be the odd individual who moved on, because – as it was tactfully put to the author on more than one occasion – 'Their face didn't fit'.

Also: Fair's Fair; Provided House; Ready For The Road

COMPETITION
One of the bizarre anomalies of the **Scotch Whisky Industry**, is that whilst competition amongst the proprietors of brands is vigorous, many of them are dependent upon each other for the perfection of their various blends. It is not uncommon for 20 or more whiskies (malt and grain) to be blended in a particular 'recipe' in the quest for the desired blended whisky. Some of the multi-nationals such as Diageo with their 27 distilleries could arguably be described as self sufficient – although they do source new make spirit and single malts from other producers to put into their blends – but the nature of the industry is such that the other producers of blended Scotch Whisky all need one another. By way of example, Pernod Ricard and also Bacardi rely upon one or more of their major competitors at Allied Domecq, Diageo, Whyte & Mackay or Edrington for grain whisky to make their own blends.

Also: Good Neighbours; Grain Distilleries

COMPUTERISATION
The author was struck by how antiquated can be the appearance of unused computerised controls now superseded by state of the art monitors and keyboards. One such example, which is deserving of Historic Scotland status, must be the former **English Electric** switching gear which used to control the grain hoppers at Balmenach.

Also: Keep Fit: Stay Happy

COMPUTERS
To see the power of computers as applied to modern-day whisky production, visit Aultmore Distillery. Here the gleaming '**Steinecker**' Lauter Tun is linked to the

[Bold text within paragraphs refers to sub-headings in the Index]

manufacturer's help desk in **Germany** and when any teething problems arise, control can be handed over to Germany – 'at the click of a mouse' (source: John Dewar & Sons Ltd).

Also: Minimal Staffing

COMPUTER TECHNOLOGY

There can be few production units nowadays which do not use computers at some stage in their day to day business. The whisky industry is no exception. A distillery such as **Braeval** (formerly Braes of Glenlivet and constructed 1972 – 1973) was actually designed and built to be run by a single operator. Some two years later **Allt a' Bhainne** was built to the same principle and all this, approximately ten years before the advent of Sir Clive Sinclair's personal computer. Today, Scapa Distillery is reopening with a full-time complement of three permanent staff.

CONDENSERS

In the past, the **vapours** from the neck of the pot still would pour through a coiled copper tube or **worm**. Located in a massive tank of cold water, the worm acted as a basic cooling device, condensing the vapours to produce the necessary spirit. This was a process which had barely changed over the centuries. However with the modernisation of distilleries in the late sixties and early seventies, combined with a rash of new distilleries, a number of companies realised that the same function could be performed by **shell and tube condensers**. The big advantage of the latter was that they took up less than half the space required by a worm. For reasons best known to themselves, certain distilleries, having made the change-over, reverted to the traditional worm (source: Forsyths Group, Rothes).

Also: Moby Dick; Worms

CONNOISSEURS CHOICE

Gordon & MacPhail's range of malt whiskies is, today, one of the easiest ways for the aficionado to sample some of Scotland's rarest drams.

CONTINUITY
Whilst certain distillery companies do introduce changes in the manufacturing process, (albeit after much careful scrutiny) one aspect that remains almost inviolate is the shape and size of the copper stills. In the case of **Ardbeg** Distillery, these have been renewed to the exact specifications of the originals of 1842 (source: distillery visit).

Also: Copper – But Why?; Still Life

CONTRASTING LONGEVITY
There remain today in Scotland, two of the oldest family distillery businesses continuing to operate from the sites where they first started: **Glenfarclas** (J. & G. Grant) and **Springbank** (J. & A. Mitchell). Both have been outstandingly successful in pursuit of their goals – each with brands much sought after around the world. The visitor is struck by how this has been achieved: the former a gleaming, modern plant, the latter almost revelling in its adherence to the traditional past, but each a testimony to the foresight of their owners and the dedication of their employees.

Also: Cleaning Routine; Foresight

CONTROL OF POLLUTION ACT
In 1974 the Government passed a law which effectively required all distilleries to obtain permission, prior to disposing of their waste into streams, estuaries and all other watercourses. This is currently 'policed' by The **Scottish Environment Protection Agency** (SEPA). The maximum fine that can be imposed if a watercourse is deemed to have been polluted, is £20,000 (source: adapted from correspondence received by the author from SEPA).

Also: Dark Grains; Effluent Into Coastal Waters;
Environmentally Friendly; Government Regulations

[Bold text within paragraphs refers to sub-headings in the Index]

COOPERAGE
Speyside Cooperage at Craigellachie is one of the few remaining in Scotland. Here they reassemble imported staves to make 'new' casks, carry out repairs to some 80,000 – 100,000 old casks per annum and, from time to time, participate in research into new techniques involving the treatment and storage of whisky. They even had a request to construct a **square cask** in the hope that this might provide a solution to more efficient warehousing (source: site visit).

Also: Flaggin; Pallets

COOPERS
Few distilleries now employ their own coopers. Some distilleries such as **Balmenach** and **Invergordon** continue to retain certain of the skills, sufficient to undertake basic repairs to casks. Qualified coopers undergo a rigorous four year **apprenticeship** 'in situ'. (source: distillery visits).
Also: Vat Builder

COPPER – BUT WHY?
Used to the exclusion of all other metals in the **fabrication** of the malt whisky **pot still** in Scotland, the inquisitive layman inevitably poses this question. Copper is not heavy. It is easily worked after heating and retains its malleability even on cooling. Hammering the metal reintroduces the hardness. It contains properties beneficial to the manufacturing process. This latter attribute is best testified to by the fact that one distillery decided to 'go modern' and substitute all copper with stainless steel. To the company's consternation, the new make spirit refused to run clear. Only after the addition of considerable quantities of **sacrificial copper** into the process, could the spirit be persuaded to run clear and the product reach the required standard. Within a year, the distillery had reverted to the more tried and tested copper (source: Forsyths Group, Rothes).

Also: Re-Cycling; Sacrificial Copper; Stainless Steel; Still Life

COPPER (CATALYST)

The metal acts as a catalyst between the various acids and alcohols to produce esters, which in turn have characteristic 'fruity' or 'flowery' aromas. Copper also precipitates **lipid material**, which serves to improve the clarity of the new make spirit. It also has the added benefit that it removes some of the undesirable **sulphur compounds** e.g. dimethylsulphide. By contrast stainless steel, for example, does not offer these properties (source: G.H. Palmer, Professor of Cereal Science, Heriot Watt University; 'A Wee Dram of Whisky' in Liquid Foods International; January, 1999).

Copper has been shown to prevent the production of sulphurous off-flavours (**Dimethyldisulphide, DMDS**). It would be impossible to produce good whisky without the use of copper stills. Even the big grain distilleries place **sacrificial copper** in their stainless steel continuous stills (source: R. Ryman, Head Brewer, St Austell Brewery).

Also: Sacrificial Copper

COPPERSMITHS

This remains one of the few genuinely traditional industries in Scotland and one which continues to depend on skills handed down through the centuries. An **apprenticeship** scheme (five years) is firmly in place at Forsyths in Rothes. With the disappearance of **Blairs** in Glasgow, **Grants** in Dufftown and the substantial reduction in size of **MacMillans** of Edinburgh, **Abercrombie** of Alloa (Diageo's in-house coppersmiths) are now Forsyths' main competitor in the U.K. The '**copperies**', as they are fondly known in the North East of Scotland, continue this proud tradition (source: Forsyths Group, Rothes).

Also: Craftsmanship

CORNWALL

The **St Austell Brewery** and Callestic Cyder at Penhallow joined forces to distil Cornish Malt Whisky. Using barley grown locally, traditional floor maltings (Tuckers of Newton

[Bold text within paragraphs refers to sub-headings in the Index]

Abbot), the brewing facilities at St Austell, and the copper still at **Penhallow**, the first annual production run of some 400 litres was laid down in 2003. Maturing in bourbon butts in the brewery's warehouse (where they also store their imported rum casks) the matured whisky will be bottled straight from the barrel, un-filtered and at cask strength. Annual production of larger quantities is anticipated and future maturation may be in different wood finishes, including their own **rum barrels** (source: R. Ryman, Head Brewer, St Austell Brewery).

Also: Green Springbank

COSMETICS

A specialist company in the Highlands of Scotland is in discussion with a major British pharmaceutical company to supply limited quantities of concentrated extracts of **Pot Ale**.

The **amino acids** that can be extracted from Pot Ale are of value to the cosmetics industry. A research chemist explained to the author that amino acid molecules are small enough to penetrate the surface layer of the skin (epidermis) and that these amino acids also have the ability to chemically bind with molecules important to the cosmetic industry, such as those which impart moisture, or a silky sensation, to the skin.

It may be worth noting that our skin is made from **proteins** such as collagen. Proteins are 'built' from amino acids. Just like a necklace is a string of beads, so a protein is a string of amino acids. This further supports the interest of the cosmetic industry in amino acids, as they are not alien to the body and, as such, are highly consumer friendly (source: Pamela Fleming).

Also: Amino Acids

CRAFTSMANSHIP

There is much 'marketing talk' about the whisky industry being traditional and nowhere can this be better demonstrated than in the manufacture of the copper still. Here is a product and a manufacturing process, in which the **traditional skills** of the Scottish work-force still reign supreme in the world. **Suntory** continue to source their stills from Scotland for their distilleries in **Japan** because, although the Japanese coppersmith **Myaki** has developed machinery which can copy the Scottish craftsmanship, it proves better value-for-money to obtain the product from Scotland. One major American whiskey company, despite being only 20 miles from the US coppersmith's plant **Vendome**, found it necessary to come to Scotland to get the perfect still. Whilst **American technology** can put a man on the moon, it lacks the traditional skills to hand beat copper into the curvaceous shape of the copper still (source: Forsyths Group, Rothes).

Also: Copper; Coppersmiths; Scottish Technology

CRAIGELLACHIE DISTILLERY
The whisky from this distillery has always had a close association with '**White Horse**', the best selling blended Scotch Whisky in **Japan**. Indeed, the distillery is known locally in Speyside as The White Horse Distillery (source: John Dewar & Sons Ltd).

Also: Horse Sense; Salmon; Shipping; White Horse

CROSSED WIRES
On one of his regular distillery trips, the lorry driver was given his dram. Often this would be **new make spirit** and consequently, absolutely clear. Topping it up with water, but which in fact was more of the same, he set off in his lorry on the return journey to the nearby railway station. Unfortunately the lorry left the road and ran into a telegraph pole, breaking it in two and wrecking the cab, with the result that the driver lost his job (source: Bill Murray, Fair Isle and formerly employed at Ballindalloch Station).

Also: Ballindalloch

CUSTOMS & EXCISE
At each distillery the Excise Office housed the Excise Officer

[Bold text within paragraphs refers to sub-headings in the Index]

and his assistants, or '**Watchers**' as they were more fondly known. In the early 1980's the Government realised that they could save a lot of money by using the distillers themselves to account for revenue due – no doubt based on the successful implementation of the VAT tax collection system. **The Rayner Report** in its 'Review of Distillery Instructions', set out the new ground rules and these were implemented in 1983 (final control of the warehouses was handed over to the distillers or '**trader**', in 1987).

The upshot of this sea-change was that all **record keeping** and security was now the sole responsibility of the 'trader'. After the initial euphoria of no longer having the Excise on site, it quickly dawned on many distillery managers that this was a most onerous responsibility. The Excise could still be called upon for advice, but their presence was characterised by long periods in which they were rarely seen on the premises. The days of mutual co-existence were gone and in its place was the visiting official.

There are now only three **Excise Officers** covering all of the distilleries from Glenturret northwards* (those to the south, including Islay are supervised by other staff). Whilst these three 'northern experts' can call on assistance from other colleagues, the trio also have other duties and responsibilities which bear no relation to the whisky industry. Thanks to the diligence of the trader and the full weight of the law that can be brought to bear on miscreants, the revenue accrued by the Exchequer has barely been dented. On the other hand the demise of the Excise on site, has resulted in a considerable loss of fascinating insights into life on the plant**.

Also: CLV; Devil In The Detail; Licensed Still; Tax
* Immediately prior to 1983 there were no fewer than 121 Excise employees covering **Speyside**
** So rarely do Customs & Excise visit distilleries nowadays, that in the case of one particular distillery, the author was astonished to learn that some employees had no understanding of the role and function of the Excise Officer.

There was a young Watcher of Bowmore
Who went on to be Excise at Ardmore
But his passionate affair,
With the lass o' Balblair
Ensured that his career was no more

CUTTY SARK

The renowned blended whisky created by **Berry Bros. & Rudd Ltd** * in 1923, was named after the famous tea and wool clipper. From 1885 - 1895 she vied to be the fastest cargo ship under sail, as she rounded Cape Horn bound from Australia to Britain. One of the most popular of her masters was Captain Woodgate, who not only bred collie dogs on board, but also enjoyed roller-skating on deck. Her arch adversary on the clipper run, 'The Thermopylae', has long since disappeared into the annals of maritime history.

Also: Scots or Scotch?

* now part of The Edrington Group (known also for The Famous Grouse and The Macallan)

CYCLE OF PRODUCTION

Few distilleries nowadays operate the 3 monthly cycle of **Springbank**. Divided into 10 – 12 week units of production, this first cycle is devoted to malting all their own barley. The second 10 – 12 week cycle completes the process by mashing and distilling. With the anticipated opening of the new **Mitchell's Glengyle** Distillery in **Campbeltown**, this production pattern will require to change, because all of the malting for Glengyle will be undertaken at Springbank. The year will still be divided into 4 seasons, but instead of it being 2 malting and 2 mashing/distilling as it is now, there will be 2 malting, 1 mashing/distilling and 1 malting and mashing/distilling (source: distillery visit).

[Bold text within paragraphs refers to sub-headings in the Index]

D

DALLAS DHU DISTILLERY

Historic Scotland (the Government's department with responsibility for the conservation of the nation's historic buildings) has preserved this former distillery near **Forres**. By way of a series of audio aids and white footprints, the individual is able to walk through and understand the workings of a distillery. The distillery remains much as it was when it ceased operations in the mid 1980's. Whilst the absence of a working atmosphere in the premises is keenly felt – why don't they introduce the smells and noises so beloved of the Madame Tussaud experience? – Dallas Dhu provides an excellent opportunity to understand the essentially simple nature of the manufacturing process, at your own unhurried pace. It would appear, however, that the 'gallons to litres assistant' was clearly enjoying a dram too many, especially when helping in The Filling Store (clearly never employed at Springbank Distillery)!

Also: Metric or Imperial

DALMORE DISTILLERY

One of the more fascinating distilleries and the one that must surely give the lie to the old adage that 'See one distillery and you have seen them all.' Difficult to find at the best of times, when the A9 trunk road used to pass its entrance gates, those on the realigned A9 traffic now zoom past, knowing not what they are missing. The new visitor centre, with its signposts from the A9, will change all of this, but hopefully the personal nature of the visit will not be jeopardised.

Also: Shapes and Sizes

DARK GRAINS

There is very little wastage in the manufacture of whisky, whether it be malt or grain whisky. The distilling industry had developed from a farming activity in the 1800's and was receptive to the entrepreneurial attitudes of the commercially minded farmer. The latter realised that the waste malted barley left behind after one of the early stages of production (soaking the ground malted barley in the mash tun) made excellent **cattle-feed** ('**draff**'). The process was further refined by mixing the draff with the liquid left over after the first distillation (**pot ale**). When dried and cut up into suitable sized pellets for their livestock, the waste (now called Dark Grains) became even more nutritious.

Intriguingly, the Dark Grains produced from grain distilleries fetch a higher price than do those from the malt distilleries, because they have fewer husks in the original mix of 'mash'. In addition, the Dark Grains from grain distilleries can be fed to sheep because the copper content is lower (than that derived from malt whisky distilleries) and therefore more suitable for sheep.

*Also: Distillation; Environmentally Friendly; Farm
Diversification; Waste Treatment*

DELIVERIES AND COLLECTIONS
Ballindalloch Station was no doubt typical of many on Speyside in the 1950s and early '60s. It dealt with freight for

[Bold text within paragraphs refers to sub-headings in the Index]

Cragganmore, **The Glenlivet** and **Glenfarclas** distilleries. The deliveries and collections were made by two or three railway owned lorries and the drivers tried to organise the last trips of the day so that they were at a distillery just before five o'clock. At that time drams were issued to the workers and any visitors who happened to be there (source: Bill Murray, Fair Isle and formerly employed at Ballindalloch Station).

Also: Dramming; Puggie

DEVIL IN THE DETAIL

The Excise continue to adopt a 'fair' approach to dealing with the producers of whisky, although neither party will be the first to admit that the old style tolerance can still be found amongst the **Excise**. The producers are now responsible for keeping the records and in this respect, meticulous attention to detail is essential. The author was informed on more than one occasion, by proud Distillery Managers, that they kept their **monthly return** 'to within 0.5 litres of accuracy'. This can be treated as a figure of speech for 'all 'W1' records must be 100 per cent accurate.' Failure to do so and inability to show good reason, results in the full weight of the Excise being brought to bear: nothing changes (source: Excise Anonymous).

Also: In And Out; Indispensable; Reciprocals

DEWARISMS

With the kind permission of John Dewar & Sons Ltd., we have included one or two of the wonderful witticisms of the younger son, **Tommy Dewar** and originally published in 'Toasts, Maxims and Wisdom Compressed'. Such was the widespread reporting and publicity attached to this irrepressible salesman at the turn of the 19th century, that his quips became known as 'Dewarisms'. He seems to have lived life to the full and remarked that 'Life may be difficult, but it's the only thing worth living.'

Also: Popularity; Similarities

DIAGEO

This company owns **Gleneagles Hotel** and numerous distilleries.

Also: Most Distilleries; Queen Mary 2; Ownership

DIRECT FIRING

Traditionally, the copper stills were heated directly by coal, but in the closing decades of the 20th century some 90 per cent of distilleries have changed over to **indirect heating** using steam-filled elements within the copper still (the same principle as the element in a kettle). This method heats the wash more gently, thus increasing the life span of the still. However, the final flavour can be different, and for this reason some distilleries have declined to follow the trend. Moving from direct to indirect heating was, in many respects, a revolutionary change for the industry and one which all distillers watched over with great care and not a little apprehension (source: Forsyths Group, Rothes).

Also: Glendronach

DISTILLATION

Most malt distilleries undertake two distillations. The first of these is carried out in the **wash still** and some 40 per cent of the original volume is transformed into '**low wines**'. The remaining 60 per cent is drained off as **pot ale**. The second distillation of these 'low wines' in the **spirit still** (also called the **low wines and feints still**) transforms the low wines into the **new make spirit**. This accounts for some 15 per cent of the low wines' volume, leaving the remaining 85 per cent to be re-distilled and any waste (approximately 40 per cent) discharged as **spent lees**.

Also: Dark Grains; Waste Treatment

DISTILLATION: TIMES 2.5

Some distilleries such as **Springbank**, will distil two and a half times. By so doing, more of the lighter **vapours** can be collected, giving the whisky more fruity, ester-y flavours.

[Bold text within paragraphs refers to sub-headings in the Index]

The wash is distilled to give **low wines**. The low wines in turn are distilled to give **feints**. A mixture of low wines and feints are then distilled again and it is from this run that the middle cut is collected. Since some of the spirit has been distilled twice (low wines) and some three times (feints) it is described as two and a half times distillation (source: distillery visit).

Author's note: there are some distilleries which pursue a **triple distillation,** for example **Auchentoshan** and **Benrinnes. Springbank** Distillery also undertakes triple distillation when it produces its **Hazelburn** Single Malt. Wm. Grant & Sons' Grain Distillery at Girvan produces a triple distilled single grain whisky called **Black Barrel.**

DISTILLERIES OF SCOTLAND
The authoritative text by Moss and Hume – 'The Making of Scotch Whisky', James & James, Edinburgh, 1981 – lists approximately 880 **licensed distilleries** known to have operated since the middle of the eighteenth century. Today, the number of operating malt distilleries is currently standing at approximately 90, plus 7 grain distilleries.

Also: Ownership

DISTILLERY MOULD
Visible on the outside of most buildings in a distillery complex and in particular on the warehouses, this black **fungal growth** even attaches itself to trees, for example at Glen Grant. At a conference organised by The Moray Firth Partnership in December, 2001 a Paper given by the then Environmental Manager at Guinness UDV Ltd., noted that ethanol is the primary energy source for this black mould. One distillery manager explained that in these litigious times in which we now live, all enquiries (regarding the black mould) are referred to Head Office, because some adjacent proprietors are known to seek financial compensation when cleaning the mould from their own buildings.

Also: Stack 'em High; Warehousing

DISTILLERY VISITS

For some people, a 'tour of a distillery' has now become a question of deciding in advance, the objective of the visit. Thus if you and your friends simply want to 'see a distillery', then the highly organised visits of **Glenfiddich, Glen Grant, Glenkinchie, Glenturret** (to name but a few) are for you. The tight schedule of these visits in the peak summer months, does mean that whilst questions are welcomed, they are often tactfully dealt with at the end, during the tasting of the local 'dram'.

By contrast, if your objective is a wider insight into the general industry, perhaps using a specific distillery as the example of how a distillery and the wider industry 'work', then the author would encourage you to seek out the less publicised distilleries. Unlike the category above, you now need to make an appointment by telephone to visit distilleries such as **Aberlour, Balblair, Balmenach, Glen Moray, Isle of Jura** (to list a number at random).

The success of some distilleries in entertaining the public and the unquestionable marketing opportunity presented by high volume visitor throughput, has led to this distinction. Hopefully the industry will continue to be able to cater for both types of visitor.

Also: Visitor Centres

DO DHEAGH SLÀINTE

Your reply to **slàinte mhath** – pronounced respectively: 'do yo slantche' and 'slantche va': Cheers!

DOMESTIC DISRUPTIONS

A useful source of information for the **Excise** would come from households intolerant of the bread-winner returning home from a day's work 'the worse for wear'. Furthermore, as Miss Birnie of Grantown-on-Spey recalled from her childhood at Aberlour and Balmenach, the side effects of easily available whisky in the distilleries resulted in the loss of her own father when she was eighteen. As one retired G.P. on Speyside

[Bold text within paragraphs refers to sub-headings in the Index]

remarked to the author, **Speyside** was recognised by the medical profession as having one of the highest incidences of cancer of the gullet in Britain.

Also: Dramming; Health; Pecking Order

'DON'T QUOTE ME, BUT..........'

In the course of the research for this book, a surprising number of very kind people who contributed and indeed, double-checked the author's facts, preferred to remain anonymous. The author's original intention to quote the source of every fact has therefore been modified.

DRAINAGE

Get this wrong at the very start of the whisky making process in the distillery and nothing one does thereafter to try to rectify matters will compensate. **Grinding** the malted barley in the mill at the distillery to the correct balance of **husks** (rough) **grist** (medium) and **flour** (fine) determines the ability of the mix of hot water and malted barley – the **mash** in the Mash Tun – to drain off every last ounce of sugars. Most distilleries will have a setting of 20-70-10 parts per 100 respectively, but each distillery will watch carefully how the drainage of the mash through the perforated plates at the bottom of the Mash Tun is performing. The ratios will be set specifically for their own Mash Tun requirements. Too much flour and the drainage 'locks'. Too many husks and the drainage is too rapid, resulting in not all of the sugars being leached out. The old traditional cast iron Mash Tuns with their perforated brass plates required constant monitoring, because the holes tended to wear. Stainless steel plates in the modern Mash Tuns are less prone to wear and tear (source: Dennis Malcolm, Balmenach).

Also: Important Stages

DRAMMING

Up until the late 1970's it was a regular practice at distilleries for drams to be issued to male employees at least once per day.

Some Managers saw fit to make the issue three times daily, with dirty or awkward tasks often meriting the bonus of a dram. Even the road tanker drivers were eligible. The original idea behind this benevolence was a belief on the part of management that it would reduce pilfering. However, a combination of circumstances led to the abolition of the scheme, not least, a concern for safety at work; concerns expressed by **Doctors' Medical Practices** in distilling areas such as Speyside, and the general shift in society's awareness of the impact of excess **alcohol** – as expressed for example, in the drink-driving legislation being introduced at that time. Most employees now receive a **free bottle** per month.

Also: Ballindalloch; Domestic Disruptions; Health; Tiring Work

DUCKS
The Arran Distillery Manager, Gordon Mitchell, has (so far as is known) the only collection of rare ducks and peacocks living within the grounds of a distillery (source: Isle of Arran Distillers Ltd).

Also: Ewan McGregor

DUFFTOWN
The local ditty indicates why Dufftown can justifiably claim to generate more capital per head of population than any other settlement in the UK – 'Rome was built on seven hills; Dufftown was built on seven stills'. These are **Dufftown, Glendullan, Mortlach, Pittyvaich** (mothballed), **Glenfiddich, Balvenie** and **Kininvie** (conveniently replacing **Convalmore** as the seventh).

DUNNAGE WAREHOUSES
The old and traditional warehouses, with their thick stone walls and earth floors, foster a **stable temperature** with fluctuation no greater than six degrees Celsius. A distillery such as Glenfarclas, has no fewer than thirty such warehouses with the maturing casks stacked three high (source: J. & G. Grant).

Also: Indispensable; Warehouse Temperature

[Bold text within paragraphs refers to sub-headings in the Index]

DUTY FREE

Spotted by the author in the Duty Free Shop of Warsaw International Airport on 6th November, 2003: **Glen Edwards'** single malt from Leith Distillers Ltd. The label stated this to be 'A Highland Malt Scotch Whisky, distilled and matured in Scotland'. Complete with a 'Royal Warrant' on the label, these 70cl bottles were on sale for the Sterling equivalent of approximately £4.

Also: Queen Mary 2

E

EARLIEST DISTILLERY (in Scotland)
The Scotch Whisky Association notes that the earliest reference to a distillery in the Scottish Parliament, is in 1690, with the mention of **Ferintosh** Distillery near Dingwall.

ECONOMICS
In 2002 The Scotch Whisky Association reported that exports of Scotch Whisky had once again exceeded £2 billion for the tenth successive year and were standing at £2.3 billion.

EDRINGTON GROUP LTD
One of the key 'independent' Scottish whisky producers, this company includes such brands as **Highland Park**, **The Macallan**, **Cutty Sark** and **The Famous Grouse**. As Pip Mills pointed out in The Whisky Magazine, Issue 31 May, 2003, the company is in fact 'largely owned and controlled' by **The Robertson Trust**. This Trust was established in the early 1960's by three Scottish ladies and continues to plough considerable sums – '£25 million over the last five years' – into good causes within Scotland.

Also: Bank of Scotland

EELS
The desire on the part of some distilleries to make maximum use of their waste energy has spawned numerous schemes – from tomatoes at **Glengarioch** to assisting heating the swimming pool at **Bowmore**. Small trout were reared at **Tamdhu** and to cap it all, eels at **Tomatin**, both using waste warm water from the manufacturing process. This latter activity had to stop when declining whisky production interrupted the supply of warm water to the tanks. At weekends, when production was halted, the eels could not

[Bold text within paragraphs refers to sub-headings in the Index]

survive the extreme differences in temperature, especially during the winter months (source: distillery visit)

Also: Swimming Pool

EFFICIENCY

Distilleries must rank amongst the most efficient production units in Britain and nowhere more so than in the far flung corners of the Scottish islands. Here, the additional **transportation costs** encourage the distillers to seek the highest possible returns when converting their malted barley into alcohol. A tonne of malted barley delivered from a mainland maltings to an island distillery, is currently about 35% more expensive than the same delivery to a distillery on the mainland (source: distillery visits).

Also: Innovative Welsh; Yield

EFFICIENCY MEASUREMENT

The unit for measuring the productive efficiency of a distillery is the litres of alcohol produced from a tonne of malted barley. Thanks to a variety of factors, not least the constantly improving quality of barley, the approximate 385 litres achieved some twenty years ago has now increased to approximately 405 – 415 litres of **alcohol per tonne of malted barley** (source: distillery visit to Ardbeg).

Also: Yield

EFFICIENCY versus TRADITION

Scrape the surface of the whisky industry and one reveals the dichotomy of an industry steeped in tradition, but at the same time, at the very cutting edge of technology. Whereas some distilleries use machine cut peat to flavour their malted barley in the kiln, Laphroaig persists in **hand cutting the peats** (some say a better 'burn' is obtained). This traditional and back-breaking task sees the distillery workforce cut some 400 tonnes per annum – wet weight – (source: Laphroaig Distillery).

Also: Coppersmiths; Kiln Drying; Lauter Tun; Peat

EFFLUENT

The distilleries on Islay and Jura, with approval from The **Scottish Environment Protection Agency (SEPA)**, are now able to transport their effluent by road tankers to a discharge pipe above Port Askaig. The pipe has been bored underground and emerges on the sea-bed, mid-channel between the two islands, where the tidal currents in The **Sound of Islay** proceed to disperse the effluent. However, some might argue that this environmental solution to comply with the regulations policed by SEPA has simply created another environmental problem. The lorries now have to travel significantly further over narrow country roads which are not suited to greater volumes of heavy traffic.

Also: Coastal Effluent; Waste Treatment

EFFLUENT INTO STREAMS AND RIVERS

Biological treatment works handle the trade effluent generated at a distillery, or on behalf of a group of distilleries. These treatment plants reduce the nature of the effluent to an acceptable limit prior to it being discharged into the nearby watercourse. Similar controls apply to surplus cooling waters, which eventually must be discharged to a nearby stream (source: adapted from correspondence received by the author from SEPA).

Also: Control Of Pollution Act

ELEGANCIA

A light and elegant single malt from Macallan. As the label on the bottle states: 'Created by skilfully selecting casks that have combined both rich, dark Oloroso and light, crisp Fino sherries'.

Also: Glendronach

EMPLOYEES

The industry in Scotland currently employs approximately 11,000 directly and some 29,000 indirectly.

[Bold text within paragraphs refers to sub-headings in the Index]

EMPLOYMENT

Automation has resulted in many distilleries operating with very few permanent staff. For example, a distillery such as Scapa on Orkney operates with only three permanent staff. Nevertheless, much depends upon the actual activities being performed at any one particular distillery. Thus for example, **Glenfiddich Distillery** employs 180 permanent staff on site (source: distillery visit).

EMPRESS OF AUSTRALIA

At Glenfarclas Distillery, the interior walls of one of its rooms are lined with the wood panels from this magnificent ocean liner. In the year 2000, the then proprietor of the nearby **Archiestown Inn**, Michael Bulger, discovered a secret compartment in a chest of drawers which he had purchased from an Inverness saleroom. Inside this drawer were the original 'blueprints' of the liner, built some 87 years previously (source: J. & G. Grant).

Also: Trains and Boats and Planes

'ENFANTS TERRIBLES'

Some (in the industry) have said that Gordon, Simon, Mark, Jim and Andrew of Bruichladdich Distillery fame would fit the bill. Others would not hesitate to include John Glaser of 'The Compass Box' whisky company in Edinburgh.

Also: Chemical Weapons

ENVIRONMENTALLY FRIENDLY

In the early 1950's, **Aultmore Distillery** successfully developed a new technique to produce a type of dried, high-protein animal feed from distillery pot ale. This plant was superseded by a Dark Grains Plant that has since closed, and the **pot ale**, and **spent grains** (draff) are now transported to the Dark Grains Plant at **Glenlossie** Distillery (source: John Dewar & Sons Ltd).

Modern **Dark Grains Plants** are subject to rigorous control by **The Scottish Environment Protection Agency**. 'The main aim of the regulations is to ensure that any emissions to the air (suspended matter and odour) are not going to be detrimental. The operators are required to keep a log of their operations and quite detailed records of maintenance etc. Failure to comply with the schedule of conditions may result in prosecution' (adapted and quoted from correspondence received by the author from SEPA).

Also: COMAH; Control of Pollution Act; Dark Grains

EQUALITY OF THE SEXES
Head for **Springbank**. Female recruits to 'Sales and Marketing' are required to do their turn at each of the production tasks (the latter being the traditional preserve, in the whisky industry, of the male of the species). At a distillery where they still malt all of their own barley (10 – 12 tons per batch and twice a week), this is no mean feat (source: distillery visit).

Also: Manageress

EQUITY
The privately owned Bruichladdich Distillery draws one third of its share-holding from residents of Islay (source: Bruichladdich Distillery Company Ltd).

Also: Octomore

EU
The European Union (including the United Kingdom) accounts for over 50 per cent of the total sales of Scotch Whisky (source: The Scotch Whisky Association).

Also: Blended Scotch Whisky; Exports

EVERY LAST DROP COUNTS
Such is the zeal of **Customs and Excise** in ensuring that all excise duties are collected, even the waste products have to be tested for their alcohol content. Their booklet 'Notice 39, 2002' clause 10.1, for example, stipulates that **fusel oil** (a

[Bold text within paragraphs refers to sub-headings in the Index]

mixture of small amounts of several alcohols produced during distillation) must be measured to ensure that it is below 8.7 per cent alcohol by volume. 'If the strength of any fusel oil is greater, the whole product is liable to duty at the spirits rate'.

Also: Balancing The Books; Customs & Excise

EVIDENCE

Draining casks exposed to sunshine was a popular means of **pilfering**, particularly if the casks were sherry butts. They often yielded substantial amounts from supposedly empty casks. A Cooper knew that one of his squad regularly indulged in this activity, and succeeded in catching the culprit with a full basin of liquid. When confronted, the employee threw the contents in the air and the evidence was gone (source: Exciseman Anonymous).

EWAN MCGREGOR

When Arran Distillery was opened in 1995 by the film star Ewan McGregor, three casks of Arran malt were laid down: one for Ewan McGregor and one each for the **Princes William and Harry** (source: Isle of Arran Distillers Ltd).

Also: Ducks

EXPERIMENTS

One of the enduring memories of the research work undertaken for this book was the frequent clash of the traditional with the innovative. At the heart of the whisky industry – both in terms of production and marketing – are direct links to the past and all that this conveys in terms of image, quality and consistency. At the same time the industry has always striven to be innovative. This can be driven by fashion, finance or by more mundane government regulations. One of the more extraordinary experiments that was mentioned, but not elaborated upon, was research into creating the necessary conditions for what was termed **synthetic warehousing**. That is to say, creating the necessary chemical reactions which would avoid the necessity to wait for the whisky to mature in a warehouse. Given current **warehousing costs** of approximately 20 pence per cask per week and assuming the not unreasonable warehousing of 100,000 casks at a distillery, this would indeed be a major breakthrough.

Also: Efficiency v Tradition; Warehouse Temperature

EXPLOSIVE

It may come as something of a surprise to the layman that the **milling process** can be associated with risk of explosion. This is particularly so with the massive factory-like mills which are a feature of the **grain distilleries**. The fine particles of dust can combine with the atmosphere to produce a lethal mixture if ignited.

Also: Giants Of The Industry

EXPORTS

In 2002, around 90 per cent of all Scotch Whisky sales were for export. It is one of the United Kingdom's top five manufactured export earners. (source: The Scotch Whisky Association).

Also: Blended Scotch Whisky; Seconds Away

[Bold text within paragraphs refers to sub-headings in the Index]

F

FAIR'S FAIR

An old Distillery Manager often said, "Even an honest man will pinch whisky" and so the **golden rule** was 'Self use, not misuse and keep it contained within the distillery community' (source: Exciseman Anonymous).

Also: Communities; Health

FAKING IT

Thanks to the boffins at **Diageo** a device has been introduced to test the veracity of the dram in your bottle. Developed for use by those such as **Trading Standards Officers** in the UK, to assist with stamping out counterfeit whisky, there may be considerable export opportunities for the gadget. In a recent television documentary, The President of the All India Distillers Association, Mr Devine Narang, was of the opinion that approximately half of all Scotch sold in **India** is fake.

FAMOUS PHEASANT

A delicious **recipe** using two pheasants: ingredients – 4 tablespoons of butter; 2 large eating apples; quarter pint of cream; juice from half a lemon; salt and pepper; half tumbler of whisky. Method: brown the bird(s) in butter; peel the apples, sauté and place the apples in a casserole with the bird(s) on top. Baste with whisky. Cook at 375 for 30 minutes, then add cream and lemon, returning to oven to cook until tender (source: George Lovie, Auchinblae).

Also: Ice Cream; Still A Restaurant

FARM DIVERSIFICATION
Many of the distilleries in Scotland owe their origins to the farmers of the 19th century who saw an opportunity to use their crops more beneficially. Today, Rockside Farm on Islay brings the wheel full circle with the creation of **Kilchoman Distillery**. This new distillery hopes to have the first bottles ready for drinking within the usual ten year span from barley to bottle. Capitalising on small is beautiful, the distillery will be undertaking all facets of production on site. Using barley from their own fields, malting, distilling, warehousing and bottling on site, the partnership of local farmer Mark French and Argyll businessman Anthony Wills aim to take production back to its roots.

Also: Dark Grains; Good Neighbours

FASHION
Whisky companies have recognised the need to promote their dram to a wider audience. The days of whisky being served with water only – and certainly not with **ice!** – are a thing of the past, witness: Glenfiddich now actively promotes 'menu cards', which include such exotics as Glenfiddich 'Zest', 'Oriental', 'Seville', 'Limelight' and 'Soho'.

Also: Mixers

FAVOURITE DRAM
Mr Nemoto Senior, a **Tokyo** bar owner and former head of The Bartenders' Association in Japan has the entire **Glenfarclas** collection in his ownership (source: J. & G. Grant).

[Bold text within paragraphs refers to sub-headings in the Index]

FERMENTATION

If you are fortunate to visit a distillery where fermentation in the old wooden **Wash Backs** has just begun, then you may be party to the sheer energy released in this process. At **Balmenach** you can sometimes feel these massive containers 'moving', as the liquid pushes and heaves against the wooden staves held in position by the sturdy iron hoops (source: distillery visit).

Also: Important Stages; Renewable Energy; Spile The Knot

FEUDS

A near neighbour to **Ardbeg** and **Laphroaig** distilleries, **Lagavulin** controlled output at Laphroaig for some sixty years. When the first owner of Laphroaig died in 1847, his son was only nine years old and so the distillery was leased to Lagavulin. In 1857 the son was now of an age where he could take over the running of Laphroaig, but Lagavulin continued as 'agents'. His brother-in-law (A. Johnston) then took over at Laphroaig (in 1877) and when he died in 1907, a court case determined that Laphroaig be inherited by Johnston's sisters. Laphroaig now felt that they were not getting a fair deal from Lagavulin (who were still acting as agents for Laphroaig) and so took Lagavulin to court and had the agency agreement terminated. So annoyed was Lagavulin that they disrupted the water supply to Laphroaig, only to lose out again in the ensuing court case and had to make good the water supply. Lagavulin then installed stills which were the same as those at Laphroaig and even went so far as to entice the Laphroaig Brewer to work for them at Lagavulin. The saga rumbled on until 1921 when the landowners of all three distilleries decided to let the distilleries buy their land. Ever resourceful, Lagavulin sought to outbid Laphroaig. They were unsuccessful and so Laphroaig and Lagavulin got down to the task of living together as harmonious neighbours (source: Laphroaig Distillery).

Also: Water

FIRST

Perhaps with some justification, the **Police** were called to be 'in attendance' at **Dalmore** Distillery, where unbiased witnesses were deemed essential in this day and age when 'My word's my bond' has passed into the annals of history. The occasion: midnight on 31st December, 1999 and the filling of five **Millennium Casks** (only the best Oloroso butts) which began one minute after midnight. As the officer(s) no doubt remarked: 'This is a first for me too' (source: distillery visit).

Author's Note: it is not recorded what the officer(s) said when they were informed that they would most certainly be offered a bottle on maturing.

FLAGGIN

Just when the cask is beginning to feel tired and in need of repair, the **cooper** will reach for his supply of American fresh-water reeds – 'flaggin' – and push these into the seams at either end of a potentially leaky cask (source: Dennis Malcolm, Balmenach).

Also: Cooperage

FLAT ON YOUR BACK

There are four flats available for use by members at the Edinburgh headquarters of The **Scotch Malt Whisky Society** (source: The Scotch Malt Whisky Society).

FLAVOUR

There is near unanimity that the quality and type of **wood** in which the whisky matures and in which it is 'finished', is instrumental in giving much of the final flavour. Whilst the experts will debate the proportions, at **Aberlour** they mention a figure as high as 70 per cent of the flavours being attributable to the nature of the cask (source: distillery visit).

Also: Ozark Mountains; Wood Sourcing

[Bold text within paragraphs refers to sub-headings in the Index]

FLIP-SIDE
Distillers are required to keep meticulous records to satisfy the requirements of **Customs & Excise**. The advantage to the distiller is considerable. They have access to one of the most exhaustive **industrial databases**. At any time senior management, scientists, analysts, researchers, blenders, engineers – anyone who has cause to query what happened at a specific time on a specific day in a specific part of the plant – has access to unparalleled information. For an industry that is a combination of **art and science** this is an invaluable databank.

Also: In And Out

FLOOR MALTINGS
The experience gained by **Gordon & MacPhail** in maturing single malt whiskies for longer periods, indicates that the finest malt whiskies held by them, were produced during the times that distilleries operated traditional floor maltings (source: Gordon & MacPhail).

FLOOR MALTINGS – TEMPERATURE
In traditional Floor Maltings, the critical necessity to control the temperature of the **malting barley** is achieved not by 'high tech' – other than the use of thermometers to monitor conditions – but instead, by a combination of three methods: turning the malting barley (using rakes and wooden shovels); varying the thickness level of the malting barley on the floor and lastly opening the windows and doors of the **malt barn** (source: distillery visits).

FLOOR MALTINGS – VOLUME
Such is the demand for malted barley from a large distillery's production process, nearly all distilleries now purchase in bulk from the modern, specialist **industrial maltings**. Of the few that continue to operate their own floor maltings, **Laphroaig**, for example, uses only 20 per cent of its own malted and kiln

dried barley, the balance coming in this instance from the **Port Ellen Maltings** on Islay. By contrast, a distillery such as **Springbank** is able to malt and kiln dry all of its own requirements for malted barley (source: Laphroaig and Springbank distilleries).

Also: Malting The Barley

FLY FISHING

The island of Islay held the 9th **European Fly Fishing Championships** from 8-12 September, 2003. It was sponsored by Morrison Bowmore Distillers Ltd.

Also: Salmon

FOG

In days gone by, the smell from **Campbeltown's** numerous distilleries was so strong that sailors could simply use their noses to guide them safely into port (source: Springbank Distillers Ltd).

Also: Campbeltown; Shipping

FORECASTING DEMAND

The whisky industry finds itself in the invidious position of having to guess consumption over a period of time. This can extend to upwards of 20 years, depending upon the brands in its portfolio that contain such statements of age. The individual producers of single malt and single grain whisky use The Scotch Whisky Association's statistics to establish **current stock**. These figures are produced yearly in arrears and issued to all its Members. These figures are of particular relevance to the **grain distillers** who have annually produced approximately 59 per cent of all whisky in Scotland over the previous twenty years*. Ironically, there is no control within the industry to curb the worst excesses of potential over-production, and so the industry moves through its characteristic cycles of varying degrees of **over-production and under production**.

Also: Changing Fortunes

[Bold text within paragraphs refers to sub-headings in the Index]

* In 2002, 370,796,654 litres of pure alcohol (lpa) of Scotch Whisky was produced. Of this total, 219,450,288 lpa (59% of total) was grain whisky production (Statistical Report 2002, Scotch Whisky Association).

FORESHOTS

Watching the new make spirit running through the **Spirit Safe** and listening to the explanation given, you may move on unaware of the interesting fact that a distillery which is seeking to utilise the **heavier alcohols**, for example **Laphraoig**, will let the foreshots run for significantly longer (approximately 45 minutes) than a distillery which is seeking to make more use of the **lighter alcohols**, such as **Ardbeg**. In the latter's case, they run the foreshots for only some 15 minutes (source: distillery visits).

FORESIGHT

One of the hazards of the Scotch whisky industry is gauging the volume and nature of demand for a product which effectively is not ready for sale until a minimum of three years after it is distilled. There can be few better illustrations of this than the excess supplies which built up in the mid 1980's, as a result of the **boom years** of expanding production a decade earlier. Few perceived the change in **consumer tastes** – the increasing popularity of malt whiskies and at the same time an upsurge in demand for wine and the 'white spirits'. But there were some who did guess correctly, and who were brave enough to take the risk. One was **Glenfarclas**. In the late 1960's they took the hitherto unheard of decision (in keeping with a similar move by **Glenfiddich**) to break out of their dependency upon blends. As a result Glenfarclas now finds itself in the somewhat unique position of having strength in depth – it can boast volume stock of single malts aged 10, 12, 15, 21, 25 and 30 years. Each of these ages is available as a core product and in addition the distillery offers a 60% abv 'cask strength' speciality, the '105' (105 British Proof, 60% abv).

Nevertheless as the distillery tour Guide informed the author, 70 per cent of production is currently still being used for blending (source: distillery visit).

Also: Changing Fortunes; New Products; Sales Projections

FRIENDS

'A friend in need ....' and you could do worse than be on good terms with distillery staff. To compensate for the tighter regulatory controls imposed by HM Customs and Excise (with the introduction of self-regulation by each distillery on behalf of 'The Excise' in 1983) most distillery companies now give all employees an annual free allocation. According to one employee based in the Inner Hebrides, 'the norm' is a bottle per month per employee. Those employed by companies with a varied selection of malts and blends, have to accept that which is deemed surplus to requirements at the time.

Also: Dramming

FRIENDS OF LAPHROAIG

This exceedingly successful **marketing** ploy has resulted to date in no fewer than 200,000 members. Mirroring the notion of 'selling' small pieces of land to Scots tracing their roots in the Highlands, 'FOL' gives qualifying members the opportunity to own and indeed visit, their own patch of Laphroaig. Since the introduction in 1993, this elite force of tipplers has reached a level of success probably unforeseen by those who indulged in the original 'brain-storming session' (source: Laphroaig Distillery).

FRISKY

Regular and random checks at **Bottling Plants** to search for pilfered whisky exiting the premises with the staff at the end of each shift invariably drew a blank. Advance warning reached the ears of the employees. The result was that the premises would be littered with all shapes and sizes of contraptions,

[Bold text within paragraphs refers to sub-headings in the Index]

containers and bottles – all empty. No animosity existed after these searches, just smiles all round (source: Exciseman Anonymous).

Also: Salad Cream

G

GARDENS
No distillery can match the 26 acres of mature landscaped gardens at Glen Grant. Established by one of the founding Grants in the mid 1880's, the Gardens were the pride and joy of 'The Major', who by the turn of the century had developed the Gardens into a life-time passion. **Chivas Brothers** has restored the Gardens to much of their former glory and, with the Back Burn tumbling through their grounds, they provide the perfect excuse for husbands to take their green-fingered partners to sample the pleasures of Glen Grant.

Also: Charcoal

GAUGING
One of the skills that has almost been lost as a result of the demise, in the early 1980's, of **Customs & Excise** on site at each distillery, is gauging. Indeed the term 'gauger' was that most commonly used for the Excise Officer.

The 'Excise' or 'Gauger' had to gauge (measure) all containers which were capable of holding liquids monitored for tax purposes. In the distillery, containers ranging from the wash backs to the spirit receivers, the casks in the warehouses, and the road tankers moving bulk whisky and new make spirit, all had to be measured. The volume, at any given level, in a new or repaired container has to be independently verified so that the Government can be satisfied that the trader is recording accurate figures.

By means of special measuring rods and tables that would seem to defy **Pythagoras**, gauging establishes accurate volume content. The dwindling number of retired excise officers trained in this skill continue to be sought after by distillers. Indeed the author has been fortunate enough to meet one

[Bold text within paragraphs refers to sub-headings in the Index]

who, with a colleague, was recently called upon to gauge stills in the Far East (source: Exciseman Anonymous).

GAY AND FRISKY
Cockney rhyming slang for whisky.

GHOSTER
Some things never change and the need to maintain production and minimise losses from interruptions to production wherever and whenever possible, is as crucial today as it was in the past. All distillery managers have contacts they know they can reach in times of extreme emergency. These specialist outside contractors are committed to distillery work and can be relied upon to turn out at a moment's notice to effect essential repairs. **Reliable tradesmen** of this calibre would be required to work through weekends and, if necessary, 'do a ghoster' – the droll North East phrase which instantly conveyed that the job was of such dire emergency that the squad would be working through the night.

GIANTS OF THE INDUSTRY
There are seven **grain whisky** distilleries in Scotland and it is unfortunate that these do not provide the general public with an opportunity to undertake a distillery tour in the manner of their smaller and more 'romantic' cousins, the malt distilleries. These giant plants are the backbone of the Scotch Whisky Industry. Given that the average bottle of blended whisky contains some 60-65 per cent grain whisky, it is easy to understand their significance to the Scotch Whisky Industry. These unloveable giants are producing a volume of alcohol far in excess of the small traditional malt distilleries. For example, within the **Whyte & Mackay** group, **Dalmore** (malt) Distillery is currently producing some 3.7 million litres per annum. By contrast and only a few miles along the road, **Invergordon Grain Distillery** (also owned by Whyte & Mackay) is

producing some 30 million litres per annum of grain whisky (source: distillery visits).

Also: Grain Distilleries; Grain Whisky

GLASGOW GRIPPER

Hangover cures come in many forms, but this concoction (which requires to be taken as the 'one for the road') has a certain ring of conviction as one rolls the Scottish 'r': two shots of vodka and Irn-Bru all chased down with a live oyster.

GLENBUCKET

Never to be confused with the idyllic Glenbuchat in Aberdeenshire, this wonderous 'hooch' sustained many a Prisoner of War in the grim confines of Colditz Castle during the Second World War. No doubt useful for steeling the nerves of prisoners intent upon escape, the brew was distilled by one Pat Ferguson of The Royal Tank Regiment from a recipe of dried fruit, sugar and yeast. Tasting notes included the blunt warning: 'packs a punch'.

Also: Tunnel Vision

GLENDRONACH DISTILLERY

Tucked away in the depths of Aberdeenshire this is one of the few distilleries to retain its coal-fired copper stills (indeed the marketing of the 15 year old product currently highlights this feature)*. The present 15 year old is, to quote from the label: '100% matured in sherry casks'. According to the label, the 'scarcity of supply and greater cost, mean it is rare indeed nowadays to find a malt whisky 100% matured in sherry casks'.

Also: Elegancia; Scotch Whisky Act 1988

* As we went to print the owners Allied Domecq announced that the coal-fired stills are to be replaced.

[Bold text within paragraphs refers to sub-headings in the Index]

GLEN GARIOCH

Located in the Aberdeenshire town of Oldmeldrum and pronounced 'glen g – eerie' (two hard g's) – this single malt hails from the distillery of the same name, owned by Morrison Bowmore, a subsidiary of Suntory. The dram should not to be confused with The **Garioch Blend** – a highly respected Scottish Dance Band from The Garioch. The latter is a fertile agricultural area dominated by the famous hill called Bennachie (518 metres).

Also: Ownership

GLEN GRANT DISTILLERY

Possibly the only distillery ever to have had its own personal **Butler** – 'Biawa Makalaga'. The redoubtable Major James Grant, on one of his many forays into the African bush, had come across the orphan and taken him back to **Rothes**. Here he attended the local school and then became **butler** to the Major. Biawa continued to live in Glen Grant House until his death in 1972.

Also: Charcoal; Gardens

GLENGYLE DISTILLERY

Located in Campbeltown and completely refurbished by its new owners – J. & A. Mitchell (of Springbank repute) – this distillery dating from 1873 recommenced distilling in 2004. Although housed in the old Glengyle Distillery buildings, none of the original equipment remained. It is in effect, a new distillery (the first of the millennium!) and is called **Mitchell's Glengyle** (source: distillery visit).

GLENLIVET (Usher's Old Vatted ....)

Usher's Old Vatted Glenlivet is generally considered to be the **first-ever brand** of Scotch Whisky. It was introduced in 1853 (source: Charles MacLean in The Scotch Malt Whisky Society Newsletter spring 2003).

Also: Popularity; Usher Hall

GLEN MORAY DISTILLERY

One of the three distilleries owned by Glenmorangie plc., this one is located unobtrusively at the western side of Elgin. With its speciality of finishing in white wine barrels (Chardonnay and Chenin Blanc), it is at the vanguard of innovation within the industry. Whilst some purists may raise an eyebrow at the seeming novelty of this approach to maturation, there is every likelihood that the white wine finish will prove as popular with consumers as the red wine finish pioneered by its sister distillery at Tain.

Also: Wine

GLEN TURNER

Such is the controlling influence of The **Scotch Whisky Act 1988** – prohibiting the naming of Scotch Whisky as any product other than one having been made in Scotland to the specific terms laid down in the Act – that the French company **La Martiniquaise** has deemed it necessary to transfer all its production from France to **Livingston**. Its new production facilities, some 30 km west of Edinburgh, will now permit its highly successful malt (and its blends) to be marketed under a label '**Made in Scotland**'.

Also: Scotch Whisky Act 1988

GLENTURRET DISTILLERY

Now 'home' to **The Famous Grouse**, this distillery was in the 1990's at the peak of its reputation for some of the most memorable corporate hospitality evenings. One of the distillery's former cats, 'Towser', is recorded by The **Guiness Book of Records** as having killed 28,899 mice in its lifetime.

GOING, GOING ....

'Never invest in a going concern until you know which way it is going' said **Tommy Dewar**, younger son to the illustrious John Dewar (source John Dewar & Sons Ltd).

GOLDEN EAGLES
During the construction of **Arran Distillery**, work was halted for several weeks to allow the two Golden Eagles, which nest in the mountain behind the distillery to give birth to their chicks (source: Isle of Arran Distillers Ltd)

GOLDEN PROMISE
The name of a somewhat unique type of barley previously favoured by distillers for the intensity of the flavours it produces, but now rarely used due to low yield of grain and low yield of **alcohol** from the malted barley. Nevertheless, The Macallan continues to use some 20 – 25 per cent of Golden Promise in its total mash and their own fields of the crop can be seen around the distillery depending upon time of year and field rotation (source: distillery visit). The Macallan is in the exalted company of the Caledonian Brewery in Edinburgh, which also uses this type of barley (exclusively) as it has just the right proportion of starch and low levels of nitrogen making it ideal for brewing.

Also: Malted Barley; Hordium Distichon

GOOD NEIGHBOURS
The origins of the distilling industry are in many respects rural, as opposed to urban, and many early distilleries were associated with farmers. In the course of his research, the author was struck by the extent to which a number of Distillery Managers continue to practise that most cherished of rural values: assisting one's neighbour. Whilst the advent of the multi-national conglomerates may have diminished this goodwill, specific areas and circumstances continue to ensure that, despite being serious competitors, a number of distilleries are only too happy to go to one another's assistance. On Orkney, Scapa Distillery has been mothballed since 1997, but every two years the staff from rival Highland Park Distillery fired up the stills and produced enough new make spirit to replenish stocks. Even

within the 'urban' context of Campbeltown, we can find Springbank Distillers Ltd assisting their competitors, The Loch Lomond Distillery Company, to get the former **Glen Scotia** Distillery re-started. There are not many industries in today's 'dog eat dog' competitive market place, where such attitudes prevail.

Also: Competition

GOVERNMENT REGULATIONS

There can be few Government departments which can vie with the Inland Revenue and Customs & Excise for being the distillers' 'bogeymen', but ask the average distillery manager for suggestions and it is almost certain that 'SEPA' will be muttered, closely followed by **The Health and Safety Executive** (HSE). **The Scottish Environment Protection Agency** can be summed up in layman's terms as the Government's pollution control department. All would agree that society is the better for having an environment largely free of contaminating pollutants. Nevertheless, it tries the patience of the most tactful of distillery managers to have to teach the young SEPA staff how a distillery works, only for them to return a few weeks later and impose the latest regulations because of the 'what if' scenario. One distillery manager was instructed to carry out a **Risk Assessment** of the trains running along the nearby railway line, in case one came off the track and threatened the distillery.

Also: Health & Safety Executive; Waste Treatment

GRAIN

This is one of the basic ingredients used in the making of whisky. In particular it is barley which is used to make malt whisky. By contrast, **grain whisky** uses a combination of varying quantities of **barley, maize** and **wheat** (source: The Scotch Whisky Association).

Also: Hordium Distichon; Golden Promise

[Bold text within paragraphs refers to sub-headings in the Index]

GRAIN DISTILLERIES

In Scotland this type of distillery provides the bulk of the volume to create the blends that are the backbone of the Scotch Whisky Industry. There are seven such distilleries in Scotland with one in the south at **Girvan** (Wm Grant & Sons) and another in the north at **Invergordon** (Whyte & Mackay). Diageo* owns 2.5 of the seven, sharing The **North British** Grain Distillery with The Edrington Group whilst Allied Domecq owns **Strathclyde**. The Loch Lomond Distillery Company owns **Loch Lomond** (dual purpose malt and grain). That of Wm Grant & Sons at Girvan lays claim to being the largest and most modern in Europe. Two of the larger conglomerates (Pernod Ricard and Bacardi) do not have access to their own grain distilleries in Scotland.

Also: Invergordon Distillery

* Diageo owns **Port Dundas** and **Cameronbridge** Grain Distilleries

GRAIN WHISKY

At the very cutting edge of using this spirit is the highly innovative and fledgling whisky company **The Compass Box** (established by John Glaser). With its new blended grain whisky called 'Hedonism' – considered by The Malt Advocate Magazine to be a rare instance of grain whisky being taken seriously – the scope for using grain whisky more adventurously is there for others to develop.

Also: Single Grain Whisky

'GREEN' SPRINGBANK

Matured in **rum** wood, these particular casks were bottled in 1991 under the Cadenhead label, but had actually been distilled in 1973. The end result from these particular casks was to produce this marvellous 'greenish tinged' malt. Although by no means widespread, the practice of using rum casks was and is not uncommon in the whisky industry. It is only recently, however, that whisky has been identified as 'rum-matured' at the time of bottling (source: distillery visit).

Also: Cornwall

GRIST TO THE MILL

Many visitors to a distillery will tend to gloss over this initial and critical part of the process, not least because of the impact of the brightly burnished copper stills at the end of a visit. Try to take the opportunity to look more closely at this part of the process and if you are fortunate enough – compare the old traditional English **Porteus** or **Boby** mills (the latter simpler and more easily maintained than the former) with the ultra-modern Swiss **Bühler** grain mills. For the traditional, visit Springbank and for the ultra-modern, visit Glenfarclas. Each is set to a hair's breadth precision, in order to obtain the desired mix of husks, grist and flour – respectively 10-70-20 per cent to 15-75-10 per cent, or thereabouts. The exact setting at each distillery is absolutely critical for the subsequent mashing process. In addition, the mill has a **de-stoner** which quite literally removes such small debris and, to cap it all, each has a magical device of magnets to catch any stray metal parts from the farmers' fields. Finally, the mill incorporates **beaters** which strip the ears off the husks to ensure maximum efficiency in the processing of the malted barley in the next phase of whisky manufacture: mashing (source: distillery visits).

Also: Milling

GUARD DUTY

The Alsatian guard dog was released from the gatehouse and had not returned to its Handler, when Police and Fire Brigade arrived in response to the automatic alarm. The Excise key-holder and Warehouse Manager attended to open the premises. Meanwhile the dog was still on the loose and, deciding to become involved, duly rounded up the Manager, the Excise Officer and two Policemen. No one was prepared to argue with the dog, when fortunately the Exciseman remembered the

[Bold text within paragraphs refers to sub-headings in the Index]

dog's name. With some coaxing, Rex relaxed his guard duties. One of the Policemen decided to pat the dog, in gratitude for its change of attitude, and was promptly bitten on the hand (source: Exciseman Anonymous).

GUNPOWDER

Before 1740, the **proof strength** of whisky (and other spirits) was established by mixing it with gunpowder. If the gunpowder flashed, then it was 'proved' that there was enough **alcohol** in the mixture. Thereafter, **hydrometers** were introduced to 'prove' the whisky (source: The Scotch Whisky Association).

Also: Proof Strength

H

HALF BOTTLE
As one Distillery Manager pointed out, you can't change human nature and so when the employee was recently found by the **Excise** to have his 'half bottle' full, the dutiful tax officers totted up his years' service and computed this against the individual's estimated consumption. The bill was presented to the distillery company and the **Exchequer** was duly reimbursed. As the Manager pointed out, he was in no position to dispute the calculation.

HANDS ON
Next time you visit a distillery and fleetingly glance at the timber used in the construction of the **wash backs**, pause a little longer and reflect upon the fact that it requires approximately twenty seven people to physically hold the staves in position. In this manner the wash back can be satisfactorily 'hooped' by the skilled coopers and their able assistants (source: visit to Ardbeg Distillery).
Also: Spile The Knot

HARD WORK
Should you ever visit a distillery and find it difficult to grasp how manually demanding an industry this can still be, visit **Springbank**. Here, the workforce on a typical two-man, 8 hour shift continues to shovel, turn and barrow the full 22 tons of malt (per week) and this over a 7 day week (source: distillery visit).
Also: Maltings

HEAD OVER HEELS
'One of the station's lorries used to deliver goods to Tomintoul and all the places around the **Braes of Glenlivet** where illicit

[Bold text within paragraphs refers to sub-headings in the Index]

distilling was not unknown. The particular driver who did that run had family connections in the Braes. We used to say that his lorry knew its own way back to the station. The driver would come into the station office, where he would empty the money out of his pockets, together with crunched up sheets of paper with all the parcel details he had collected. One particular night he dropped some money on the floor and, bending down to pick it up, fell clean over on his head. It sounds unbelievable when I think back' (source: Bill Murray, Fair Isle and formerly employed at Ballindalloch Station).

HEALTH

Drinking in moderation can be beneficial. This has been endorsed in a report by the **British Medical Association**, which states that up to 30 grams of **alcohol** a day – the equivalent of four single whiskies – can help protect against heart disease. Misuse can be detrimental to health (source: The Scotch Whisky Association).

Also: Domestic Disruptions; Dramming; Pipe Dreams

HEALTH & SAFETY EXECUTIVE (HSE)

As in so many other walks of life today, it comes as little surprise to find that the HSE's influence has reached Scotland's distilleries. Rulings from bureaucrats (many with no experience of the industry over which they are presiding) have consequences that few could foresee. An example which came to the author's attention during visits to distilleries is the HSE's insistence that the **still house** must now be vented to the outside. Prior to this ruling, any fumes from the distillation process were left to find their own way out through open windows, doors and other draught induced methods. But the HSE's insistence that vents be fitted to the stills resulted in some of the distilleries losing alcohol due to the **venturi** process effectively sucking off the spirit. Given that this was a process imposed by the HSE, one might expect the distillers to be compensated, but no!

Also: COMAH; Government Regulations; Waste Treatment

HER MAJESTY QUEEN ELIZABETH

When the Queen consented to open the **Arran Distillery Visitor Centre** in 1997, she may well have been influenced by the fact that the **Royal Yacht Britannia** had anchored in **Lochranza Bay** during her honeymoon cruise around the Western Isles (source: Isle of Arran Distillers Ltd).

Also: Ewan McGregor

HIGHLAND BOUNDARY FAULT

Used by the whisky industry to this day to help differentiate between Highland and Lowland whiskies, this geological fault line was nevertheless serving a useful purpose – albeit for the **Excise** – as early as 1793. In that year, James Armour of Campbeltown was issued with a licence for a forty gallon still. However, it only permitted him to sell his whisky north of the Highland Boundary Fault (spelt out in some considerable geographic detail in the licence). Not only was the area of sale restricted, but he could only use '**barley, bere** or **bigg**' which had been grown north of this line. To cap it all, this law-abiding citizen had to pay the sum of sixty pounds per annum, plus a deposit of almost the same sum, in case he defaulted (source: The Kintyre Antiquarian and Natural History Society Magazine, Number Four, 1978).

Author's note: the geographic restrictions were imposed by the Government in their desire to protect English producers from Lowland Scottish imports. In turn the Lowland producers sought protection from Highland imports (see: 'The Making of Scotch Whisky', Michael Moss and John Hume, James and James, Edinburgh,1981)

Also: Regional Production

HOME BREW

Head for **New Zealand** and here (as in some other countries) you can set up your own still (maximum 40 litres) and have no worries about the local Exciseman raiding the premises. Your

[Bold text within paragraphs refers to sub-headings in the Index]

necessary ingredients are purchased from the specialist home brew suppliers. According to Allan Joyce in Rotorua, most are using stainless steel to make the still – as he remarked 'a hangover from the skills and materials inherited from the dairy industry'.

HORDIUM DISTICHON

The precision required to make whisky starts with the **barley** from the farmer's field. It is this specific barley – *hordium distichon* – which is used to produce **malted barley**. Varieties such as **Chariot** and **Optic** with their low nitrogen levels (below 1.6) and high germination rate are popular with distillers. The grains require to be free of visual signs of fungal and bacterial infection because these risk contaminating the spirit during the distillation process (source: G.H. Palmer, Professor of Cereal Science, Heriot Watt University; 'A Wee Dram of Whisky' in Liquid Foods International; January, 1999).

Also: Golden Promise

HORSE SENSE

Before the **Breathalyser** was introduced, two mounted policemen daily would ride into the loading bay of a warehouse in Glasgow and partake of their morning refreshment without dismounting. They then returned to the busy Broomielaw in Glasgow for continued traffic duties (source: Exciseman Anonymous).

Also: Craigellachie; White Horse

[Bold text within paragraphs refers to sub-headings in the Index]

I

ICE CREAM

An excellent honey and whisky **dessert** – ingredients: half pint of double cream; 4 tablespoons of whisky; 3 – 4 tablespoons of thick honey; 4 egg yolks. Method: whip the cream, gradually adding the whisky until fairly thick. Warm the honey until hot and runny. Whisk the yolks, gradually pouring on the hot honey and keep whisking until thick and pale. Fold both of the mixes together and divide amongst eight or nine ramekins. Freeze and cover when their surfaces are firm. Serve straight from freezer (source: H. Beck-Slinn, Dingwall).

Also: Famous Pheasant; Still A Restaurant

IDENTIFICATION

Next time you visit a distillery and see how all plant and vessels are clearly named and identified, thank HM Customs and Excise for their considerate approach. Under **Notice 39**, 2002 clause 5.4 these must carry permanent marks, names or letters ....and all pipe-work must be clearly marked to show what they carry – water, wort, wash, low wines, feints or spirits.

ILLICIT STILLS

Captain William Fraser, proprietor of **Brackla** Distillery, complained to a Parliamentary Commission in 1821 that he was unable to sell whisky within 120 miles because of the number of illicit stills* in the area (source: John Dewar & Sons Ltd).

Also: Licensed Stills

* There is an excellent example of an original illicit copper still in the Museum of Islay Life at Port Charlotte.

IMPACT

The average reader may be surprised to learn about the impact of different types of whisky within a given blend. Invite some of your friends around for the evening and ask them to bring a bottle of **Lowland** single malt (eg. Glenkinchie); **Island** single malt (eg. a peaty one from Islay or Skye); a **Highland** single malt such as Dalmore; a **Speyside** single malt with some 'honey notes' (eg. Glenlivet) and a **Speyside** such as Strathisla for its 'grassy' overtones. You supply the bottle of grain whisky (eg. Cameron Brig or Invergordon) a calibrated syringe (100 ml capacity) and suitable glasses. Write the names of your six whiskies down the left hand column of your grid. Draw some three or four columns to the right of this. Write down 30ml in the box beside the grain whisky and keep this the same in the other boxes to the right in that row. Now decide on the type of blend you wish to make. You have 70 ml left to distribute amongst the remaining five whiskies. So, if for example you wished to have a quite peaty blend, you might allocate Islay 15ml; Lowland 5ml; Highland 15ml; 'Honey' 15ml and 'grassy' 20 ml. Write whatever numbers you decide upon into the appropriate row in the first column and, using the **syringe**, squirt into one glass the requisite volume. Repeat the exercise trying this time to make a less peaty Blend and don't forget to write your figures into your matrix. The fascination lies in realising the impact which a very slight change in only two or three of the six whiskies will have upon any variation you care to make (source: with fond memories of lessons learned at the hands of Colin Scott, Master Blender, Chivas Brothers).

Also: Blending; Players and Managers

IMPORTANT STAGES

As the industry strives to increase its efficiency, researchers find themselves analysing every facet of production and as one soon-to-retire Distillery Manager put it: 'Telling us what we could have told them years ago'. For example, the

[Bold text within paragraphs refers to sub-headings in the Index]

fermentation process – to quote from the words of Professor G.H. Palmer, Heriot Watt University, 'A Wee Dram of Whisky' in Liquid Foods International; January, 1999 – 'is one of the most important stages in the production of Scotch whisky'.

The objective is to ferment the liquid extract (the **wort**) from the **malted barley** to produce a large quantity of **ethanol** and a mixture of **flavour compounds**. It is the latter which hold one of the keys to whisky production. The chemical reactions taking place during fermentation produce 'esters' and it is these which have the fruity or flowery **aromas**.

Also: Drainage; Fermentation; Phenols and Processing; Yeast

IMPURITIES

In some distilleries close observation of the **spirit safe** reveals a mesh sieve. This provides an opportunity to trap any foreign matter, for example **verdigris** emanating from the interior of the copper still, prior to maturation (source: distillery visits).

Also: Copper – but, why?

IN A WORD

Are you bamboozled by the quirky descriptions of present day **tasting notes**? Then you may be one of the whisky drinkers who was enjoying a dram in the early 1980's. At that time, the newly created **Scotch Malt Whisky Society's** average 'tasting note' contained information (for example) that 'bottle Number 3.1' was 'peaty and salty'.

Ten years later and a few more descriptive words had been added to describe the contents of a particular bottle: such as 'butter and caramel'; 'nutty, like peanut brittle' and 'the aftertaste is, by contrast, very dry and astringent'.

Today, the Society's writer is likely to describe a specific bottling in terms that were unheard of twenty years previously: 'The immediate impression on the nose is perfume, with oranges and orange blossom, Maraschino cherries, sponge cake and Italian panettone. It drinks well straight (and is) sweet, but with lively acidity and traces of glacé cherries. Water introduces nuts, linseed oil and crystalline cane-sugar. The orange notes edge towards orange bitters'.

A transmogrification, and one that the Society believes their very own Gordon Smith and Pip Hills may have been instrumental in pioneering (source: with acknowledgement to Arthur Motley at The Scotch Malt Whisky Society for delving into their records).

Also: Flat On Your Back

IN AND OUT

Those of an analytical disposition and arithmetic mind may wonder how the **Government** knows that it is getting the taxes due from the spirits produced in any one distillery. In simplistic terms this is done by comparing the quantities of raw materials going in at the start with those of the finished product. The **Excise** look for any deviations from the norm and act accordingly. In so doing, The Excise has recourse to the minutiae of detail recorded at each stage of production by the distillery staff and constantly checked by management. The distillery keeps daily **Record Books** for all stages of operation including Milling, Mash-house, Tun-room, Stillhouse and Spirit Receiver/Warehouse. From these, a weekly **Compare** is produced by the distillery manager. A copy is retained at the distillery and a copy sent to the company's head office. A **Monthly Return** (form W1) of stock and movement of stock is submitted to Customs & Excise. In addition, and using the information from the weekly Compare, this is backed up by the **Quarterly Return** of distillery production (form W21). In summary, the Excise has recourse to years of records should they wish to mount an investigation.

Also: Devil In The Detail; Flip-side; Password

INDISPENSABLE

This can be the only word to apply to the **Warehouseman** at **Tomatin**, who is in charge of the 16 warehouses. When the

[Bold text within paragraphs refers to sub-headings in the Index]

Distillery Manager requires to find a particular cask it is quicker for him to ask this employee of some 30 years standing to consult his pocket books, rather than 'firing up' the computer (source: distillery visit).

Also: Dunnage Warehouses; Warehousing

INFLATION

When asked how much it would be to renew the specially shaped 'half cut-away' glass containers in the **Spirit Safe**, the Manager at Balmenach was informed by their regular supplier 'about £30'. When the order was collected the price had doubled. Accustomed to a then current rate of inflation of 4 per cent, he was informed that the precise price could only be given once they had counted all the failed attempts to 'break the glass along the desired lines'!

INNOVATIVE WELSH

Gwalia Distillery in Penderyn, South Wales requires only a single **copper pot still** for the purpose of distilling. Given that the Scots traditionally use two and the Irish three, this would indeed seem to be pushing the frontiers of 'the cratur' to new horizons. This remarkable breakthrough relies upon some 24 sieve plates positioned in the neck above the pot, and the still also has the necessary facility to re-cycle vapour (as in the common **reflux** action of the traditional pot still in the Scottish distilleries).

The spirit is normally drawn off at the seventh plate, but the weight and the style of the end product can be altered and influenced by changing the number and position of the sieve plates.

The single still which was developed by a team led by a Dr David Faraday would appear to be much more **energy efficient**, consuming only 38 per cent of the energy needed to power the traditional (Scottish) pot stills. At a time when all distillers are striving to find economies of production, this is no small consideration.

INVERGORDON DISTILLERY

Owned by **Whyte & Mackay Ltd** (formerly **Kyndal Spirits Ltd**) this 'powerhouse' of a distillery makes **single grain whisky** and does all blending for the parent company on the same site. It has its research and quality control laboratories on site and a large **Dark Grains Plant** for the treatment of the waste from this distillery. The waste from the company's malt distilleries is not treated here. In addition, the distillery has its own **cooperage** for repair and maintenance and also for **de-char/re-charring** of casks. The sheer productive capacity of **grain distilleries** is encapsulated by the extensive warehouse storage of their output. Invergordon is currently warehousing some 700,000 casks of whisky. The lasting impression could not be further from the traditional malt whisky distillery. There are only seven grain distilleries in Scotland, but they are currently producing some 59 per cent of all whisky made in Scotland (source: distillery visit and The Scotch Whisky Association Statistical Report 2002).

Also: Forecasting Demand; Grain Distillery; Ownership

IRISH WHISKEY

By definition this is distilled and matured in Ireland. In the case of **Pot Still** whiskies, Irish Whiskey distillers tend to favour three distillations rather than two, as is general in Scotland. The range of cereals used in Ireland is greater than that used in the making of Scotch Whisky (source: The Scotch Whisky Association).

ISLAY AND JURA

The two islands are home to eight distilleries. They are producing in excess of 20 million **litres of alcohol per year** and with a current rate of duty of £19.56 per litre of alcohol, these two islands can claim to be significant contributors to the Government's purse (source: Islay and Jura Visitor's Handbook; Islay and Jura Marketing Group, 2003).

Also: Tax

[Bold text within paragraphs refers to sub-headings in the Index]

ISLAY MALTS

Only a small proportion of the whisky distilled on Islay is actually matured on the island, the majority being removed for maturation in warehouses in Central Scotland (source: Bruichladdich Distillery Company Ltd).

ISLAY MIST

A blended whisky created in 1928 specifically for the coming of age of the Laird's son at Islay House. The Laird, concerned that Laphroaig might be too heavy for everyone's taste, asked the then distillery proprietor – Ian Hunter – to make a suitable blend (source: Laphroaig Distillery).

ISLAY PILLAGED MALT

This exclusive, vatted Ten Year Old Islay Malt was a 'one-off' bottling by Bruichladdich Distillery in 2003. It has extraordinary origins. Islay is justifiably proud of its strenuous **fund raising** events for local and national charities. The distillery companies on the island are equally renowned for their generosity in contributing to numerous local good causes. This particular vatted 10 year old stems from the exertions of a team of rowers (mostly distillery employees) who, over 4th and 5th July 2003 rowed around the island's distilleries. They collected 25 litres of matured whisky from each distillery and the 175 litres were vatted prior to bottling at the new **Bruichladdich Bottling Plant**. The resultant 'haul' (no pun intended) of approximately 250 bottles was auctioned off and raised £25,800 for charity (source: Ileach).

Also: Three Sheets In The Wind

ISLAY SINGLE MALTS

The highly individualistic – some might even venture to suggest 'cult' – whiskies from this west coast island are experiencing considerable success. Although only reopened in 1997, **Ardbeg's** production has nearly quadrupled in the last seven years (source: distillery visit).

J

JAPAN

The Japanese have numerous brands of their own whisky. It is frequently drunk with copious amounts of water and in this manner it is enjoyed as an accompaniment to food. The numerous city bars cater for the more serious whisky enthusiasts in the evenings. This reminded the author of the occasion when he invited a **Japanese businessman** to his house for the evening. All offers of refreshment were declined except for 'a dram'. A litre of Bell's was duly consumed – virtually unaided. Mr Yokota was propelled up to bed at midnight and was ready for a drive around Loch Ness at 0630 next day: bright as a button.

Also: Mizuwari

JAPAN IN SCOTLAND

Such is the reverence in which the Scotch Whisky Industry is held, that the Japanese have recognised the benefits of owning their own distilleries in Scotland. The following distilleries are currently in this category of ownership: **Auchentoshan, Ben Nevis, Bowmore, Glengarioch** and **Tomatin**.

Also: Ownership; Craftsmanship

JUSTICE

A Police informant warned that a whisky warehouse would be broken into on a certain night. Police and Excise were in attendance overnight without incident. During the long night, one of the **bobbies** flexed the night stick he was carrying and remarked 'We will let these boys in and make sure that they are carried out.' The break-in occurred the following night and the Police duly carried out the visitors (source: Exciseman Anonymous).

[Bold text within paragraphs refers to sub-headings in the Index]

K

KEEP FIT: STAY HAPPY

Just ask the staff at **Balmenach**! No doubt in order to stay fit enough to keep the distillery spotless, the current squad asked the Distillery Manager if they could convert one of the unused buildings into a **gym**. Now everyone is happy: quite extraordinary!

Also: Queen's Silver Jubilee

KILN DRYING

The few distilleries which continue to dry their **malted barley** in a traditional 'pagoda-roof' kiln do this primarily to retain their own degree of control over the final flavour and **phenol content** of the malted barley. The main source of drying is hot air, blown up through the floor of the kiln. The more traditional method of drying over a **peat fire**, is nowadays only used to provide controlled, additional flavour. All other distilleries rely upon the **industrial maltings** (factories which make malted barley from ordinary barley) to provide them with their own specification (source: visits to maltings and distilleries).

Also: Malting The Barley; Peat; Phenols

L

LAPHROAIG DISTILLERY

'There's a thin line between love & hate. It's about one third of the way down the bottle' – one of a number of advertising slogans for this distinctive malt (source: Laphroaig Distillery)

Also: Feuds; Floor Maltings – Volume; Friends of Laphroaig; Islay Mist; Tradition

LAUTER TUN

Initial confusion may greet the visitor to more than one distillery as they grapple with Semi-Lauters, Lauters and the more prosaic Mash Tun. The latter represents the traditional container in which the milled malted barley is soaked and stirred to extract the **sugars** from the **starch** in the malt. However, given the very high initial cost of the malted barley, it is essential to try to extract the maximum amount of sugars for the next phase: fermentation (in the wash backs).

The **Semi-Lauter**, quite simply, has a more efficient drainage system and a more efficient stirring mechanism than the traditional **Mash Tun**. It has a flat bottom and so takes up less space in the restricted confines of some distilleries than does its big brother counter-part: the (full) Lauter.

With its conical shaped bottom, the (full) Lauter offers maximum efficiency in draining off the liquid from the mash (the mixture of malted barley and hot water). In addition, the mechanism used for stirring the mash can be moved up and down through the mix, thereby generating a more efficient process and so extracting the very last ounce (gram) of **sugar** from the mash. This increased efficiency of operation means that the milled malted barley can have a higher percentage of **fine flour** in the mash, so permitting the higher extraction of sugars. By contrast, in the traditional Mash Tun with its poorer

[Bold text within paragraphs refers to sub-headings in the Index]

drainage, too much of the fine flour from the milled malt would clog up the drainage and hold back some of the valuable sugars.

The fact that Semi-Lauters and Lauters are invariably made from **stainless steel** – sometimes burnished so that you can almost see your own reflection – adds to the aura of efficiency over the traditional Mash Tun (source: distillery visits).

Also: Efficiency v Tradition; Mash Tun; Stainless Steel

LAYING DOWN

Once whisky has been bottled and securely sealed, there is no further maturing, because **oxygen** in the air cannot get to the whisky (source: The Scotch Whisky Association).

Also: Angels' Share

LICENSED STILLS

The smallest size permissible under the terms of the **Alcoholic Liquor Duties Act 1979** is 1,800 litres. The logic behind setting a figure was that small stills could be easily dismantled and hidden. It is possible to gain permission from the **Commissioners** for small stills – for example stills for demonstration purposes or research.* The **licence** to operate stills within a distillery is issued free of charge (source: HM Customs and Excise, 2003).

Also: Still a Restaurant

* Drumchork Hotel in Wester Ross has recently obtained a licence for a 'licensed illicit still' – an oxymoron if ever there was one. This forms the basis for a tourist attraction, demonstrating how small stills of 40 gallons (182 litres) were successfully used to produce a decent dram.

LIME

The perceptive may note on traditional floor maltings, such as at Springbank, that in order to kill off **bacteria** between successive 3 month malting cycles a light white covering of lime coats the concrete floor of the **Malt Barn** (source: distillery visit).

LITRES

Note the difference between a litre and a **litre of alcohol**. The latter is a derivative of the percentage **alcohol strength**. Thus a case (12 bottles) of 40 percent, 70cl bottles of whisky, contains 8.4 litres of whisky, but only 3.36 litres of alcohol.

Also: Tonnes and Litres

LOST, STOLEN OR DESTROYED

Should this happen to **duty suspended whisky**, for example whilst in bond in the distillery's **warehouse**, the whisky company is held responsible for the **excise duty** due on the said goods (source: HM Customs and Excise, 2003).

[Bold text within paragraphs refers to sub-headings in the Index]

M

MACDUFF DISTILLERY
The single malt emanating from this distillery is called **Glen Deveron**.

Also: soap

MALTED BARLEY
This is fundamentally different from the **barley** which originally came from the farmer's field: for a start, it sells at approximately twice the price. It has been transformed so that it will produce a far greater yield of spirit (**ethanol**) during the fermentation stage of the whisky manufacturing process (source: G.H. Palmer, Professor of Cereal Science, Heriot Watt University; 'A Wee Dram of Whisky' in Liquid Foods International; January, 1999).

MALTING PROCESS
The harvested barley is transformed by means of a distinct three phase process into malted barley. After clearing out small stones and other field detritus, the function of **steeping** in the **saladin box** is to produce a strong uniform growth in the grain. The **germination** phase is when the **enzymes**, vital for converting the **starch** into **fermentable sugars**, are produced. Finally, the **kilning process** involves drying the **green malt** to halt the germination and reduce the moisture content, but most importantly, to preserve the **enzymes** released during germination. It is these crucial enzymes which subsequently drive the final conversion of **starch** to **fermentable sugars**, during the mashing process at the distillery (source: visit to Bairds Malt Ltd).

MALTINGS
Industrial factory-like complexes now dominate the supply of

malted barley to the whisky industry. Prior to the 1970's the supply was either drawn from the small individual distillery maltings on site, or, alternatively, transported north from malting plants in England. **Moray Firth Maltings** (now part of **Bairds Malt Ltd**) was a classic example of this transfer of production north. Within 2 – 3 years of setting up their first factory in the Moray Firth area, the four enterprising ex-employees of a Lincolnshire maltings company, had doubled their capacity. Today, approximately half their production is for the whisky industry and the balance for the brewing industry. (source: visit to Bairds Malt Ltd).

Also: Hard Work; Storage Capacity

MALTING THE BARLEY

A common misconception for the lay distillery visitor is that **barley** is mixed with **malt extract**, but as G.H. Palmer, Professor of Cereal Science, Heriot Watt University explains in his excellent paper 'A Wee Dram of Whisky' in Liquid Foods International; January, 1999, this is not the case. The farmer's barley goes to the **Maltings** (the name given to this particular industrial plant or factory)* where, by a process of soaking and **germination** – all carefully controlled for temperature and humidity – the grains are encouraged to grow to a point where the plant hormone, **gibberellic acid**, is produced. This hormone induces certain **enzymes** which are instrumental in breaking down the starchy **endosperms** in the barley. The release of this **starch** and certain **proteins** changes the farmer's hard barley into a softer and (once dried) more friable grain. It is this altered grain which is called **malted barley**. During the **drying process**, complex chemical reactions take place and it is at this stage that the characteristic **flavour compounds** of **malt extract** are produced – important precursors of **whisky flavour**. In addition, each distiller specifies the degree to which they wish the **drying process** to be influenced by **peat**.

Also: Floor Maltings – Volume; Raw Material Costs

[Bold text within paragraphs refers to sub-headings in the Index]

MANAGERESS

Very few distilleries have ever had ladies in senior positions. In an industry which traditionally involved considerable manual labour, working one's way up through the ranks would have been an arduous task. Notable exceptions include Miss Nicol the manageress at **Glenburgie** Distillery in the late 1930's and Miss Bessie Williamson, Owner and Managing Director at **Laphroaig** from 1954 – 1972 (source: Gordon & MacPhail's Distillery Profiles and Laphroaig Distillery).

MARRYING

If you are lucky, when you are on a distillery tour, mention may be made of this key part of the process which takes place between the manufactured **new make spirit** and the bottle. Unless you are on a special tour it is unlikely that anything further will be explained. At the risk of grossly over-simplifying a process that has almost as many variations as there are distilleries, marrying can be considered a key part of the blending process. *

Different matured (or maturing) whiskies are mixed to give the desired end result: a product ready for bottling. The generalisation stops there, when one realises that blends are married; single malts are married and mature whiskies are married. The mix is undertaken in a variety of different sized containers, for example 2,000 litre – 100,000 litre containers (often called **tuns** or **vats**). All blenders agree that there is no set period within which the marrying should take place: it can be from one week to months. But make no mistake, this is a vital stage on the route to the bottle and sadly one about which very little is heard on a distillery visit.

* With thanks to Whisky Magazine, May 2003 and the fascinating article by Ian Wisniewski.

Also: Blending

MASH TUN

Here is the container which, with the aid of hot water, sieves out all the goodness from the **malted barley**. The objective is to obtain – in liquid form (the **wort**) – the nutritious extract of **sugars**, **amino acids**, **vitamins** and **minerals** (source: G.H. Palmer, Professor of Cereal Science, Heriot Watt University; 'A Wee Dram of Whisky' in Liquid Foods International; January, 1999).

Also: Lauter Tun

MASTER BLENDER

Those with the **nose** and who have the required 'attributes' are accepted into the blending team. From that stage onwards it may take approximately ten years of 'nose-on' experience to reach the revered status of Master Blender. The function of the **blending team** is critical in retaining consistency of products and also in developing new brands (source: Colin Scott, Master Blender, Chivas Brothers).

Also: Aged Inventory; Players and Managers

MEASLES

From Mrs Marigold MacLeod (now living in Saltash, Cornwall) comes the intriguing fact that a **Clynelish** 'dram' helped her to beat the worst effects of measles. As an eighteen year old, seriously ill with the disease and parents and doctor gravely concerned that the customary rash was refusing to develop, her Uncle John announced, 'I'll soon sort you out'. Returning half an hour later with a bottle of clear liquid, from which he poured out a small glass-full, he instructed the teenager – now past caring – to 'Drink that'. Within ten minutes, she was bright red from head to foot and went on to make a rapid recovery.

Also: Antidote; Toddy

[Bold text within paragraphs refers to sub-headings in the Index]

METRIC OR IMPERIAL

Springbank is a wonderful confusion of the two; dictated not by the age of its employees, but by the age and type of its equipment. What better illustration of an industry that looks both to the present and to the past for its inspiration (source: distillery visit).

Also: Age; Tonnes and Litres

MICROWAVES

This technology might more probably be expected to have an application in cooking the employees' lunch at the distillery. It is, however, being applied to a critical part of the production process: **maturation**. In a major, long term experimental programme involving numerous partners, the technology is being applied to treat the inside of the oak barrels and casks used for maturation. The idea is to try to replicate the traditional **charring**.

Perhaps spurred on by the realisation that the heavy reliance upon American Bourbon casks might one day have to be replaced by oak casks from other sources, there emanated the need to find an efficient method to replicate the charred inside of the **bourbon cask**.

Whereas the inside surface of a newly charred or re-charred cask will display a definite rough surface (it reminded the author of the larger embers left in an incompletely burned pile of logs) a surface subjected to the microwave treatment is smooth. The contrast could hardly be starker. The experiment is approximately half-way to completion, and one of Scotland's largest cooperages has its 'Microwave' machinery safely stored, in anticipation of a successful outcome. Masami Onishi writing in The Scotch Malt Whisky Society Newsletter, Winter 2003, notes that 'Old casks of excellent quality (at **Hakushu Distillery**) are re-charred and re-toasted in an original method using infrared radiation for reactivation'.

Also: Charring; Toasting

MILESTONES

Inevitably, different personnel will view the various critical events of the last four – five decades according to their own perspective and responsibilities over that period. The establishment of **Glenfiddich** single malt and the demise of **direct fired stills** are two milestones often mentioned to the author. However, one long serving manager opined that the **energy crisis** of the early 1970's had his vote. As he put it, the days of **Dufftown** and **Rothes** nestling in a cloud of steam emanating from various valves, pipes and chimney stacks, rapidly became a thing of the past as each distillery frantically repaired and replaced equipment. The necessity for **energy conservation** in the early '70s, at a time when fuel was being rationed to motorists, was the precursor to the industry transforming itself into one of the most **energy efficient** in Britain.

Also: Climate Change Levy; Classic Malts

MILLING

Malted barley is ground down to produce **grist** and this is the material that is mixed with hot water in the mashing process. In order to ensure the most efficient extraction of the **fermentable sugars**, calibrated sieves are used to sort the milled malted barley into the following proportions* – 21 per cent 'husks'; 74 per cent medium grist and 5 per cent **fine flour** (source: from 'The Grain To The Glass' by J. & G. Grant).

Also: Grist To The Mill

* **Author's note:** actual figures will vary between distilleries, but are generally around these ratios.

[Bold text within paragraphs refers to sub-headings in the Index]

MINIMAL STAFFING

Many of today's distilleries are now operated by only a few staff. **Computerised controls** have come to the aid of the cost conscious accountants in the industry. For the public interested in the detail of how whisky is made, this has had one unforeseen drawback – not that the distilleries have ever been run for the greater benefit of the public. The various specialist trades have slowly but surely vanished. The **miller, mashman, brewer** and **stillman** have each been subsumed by the **shift operator**. This employee will have a full understanding of all technical details required to run each phase of production. The net result for visitors – especially where they are conducted around by a **Tour Guide** – is that they are unlikely to meet specialists, who might have been only too keen to emphasise that *their* part of the production process was the most important and, in so doing, perhaps provide some additional fascinating insights into the whisky making process.

Also: Computers

MIXERS

Whisky Mac; **Rusty Nail** or simply whisky and lemonade – fashion has moved on since 1967, when a barman in Tomintoul resolutely refused to serve the author (who was trying to impress his girlfriend) with a 'Glenfiddich and orange'. Nowadays, no more august a body than The Scotch Whisky Association produces an excellent 'forbidden fruits' card with eleven suggested whisky drinks.

Also: Fashion

MIXOLOGIST

The wonderful term given to the expert who concocts **cocktails**.

MIZUWARI

This is the expression used in Japan to describe copiously

diluting one's whisky with water to produce a long drink before and during meals.

Also: Japan

MOBY DICK

'….. the whale-line…..spirally coiled away in the tub, not unlike the **worm** pipe of a still….' (from the book of that name by Herman Melville).

Also: Worms (technical)

MODERNISATION

One of the anomalies of the whisky industry is that, whilst it purports to being traditional, it has not been afraid of pushing the frontiers of science and technology. This process was greatly aided by the advent of the large whisky conglomerates which were in a better position than the individual family owners, whom they had taken over, to consider trying new techniques. The motivation was, of course, economies of production, but nevertheless these were bold moves in an industry that did not fully understand the processes at work. Two of the biggest changes (on the production side) in the last thirty years have been the introduction of **indirect fired stills** and the introduction of the **shell and tube condenser** (source: Forsyths Group, Rothes).

Also: Milestones

MOST DISTILLERIES

Diageo owns the most malt distilleries in Scotland (twenty seven).

[Bold text within paragraphs refers to sub-headings in the Index]

N

NANCY WHISKEY

In June 1978, The Kintyre Antiquarian and Natural History Society Magazine included the eight stanzas of 'Nancy's Whisky' – also known in Scottish Folk Song circles as 'The **Calton Weaver**' (an area of Glasgow near the Gallowgate). Referring to the ·establishment which the young weaver encountered, whilst going to 'buy myself a suit of new clothes', he came to rue his encounter with her whisky –

> 'Oh, the more I tasted, the more I liked it,
> An' the more I liked it, I tasted more,
> An' the more I tasted, the more I liked it,
> Till all my senses were gone ashore'

This folk song actually created the real-life legend of a famous **Scottish Folk Singer** of the early 1950's – Nancy Whiskey (note the Irish spelling in her name). Born Anne Wilson in Glasgow in the 1930's , she adopted this 'nom de chanson' because she was associated with singing the song on the folk circuit. However, her most famous rendition was that of 'Freight Train', reaching the top of the UK charts in the late '50's. Most of the rest of her life was spent in England, where she lived with her husband and daughter. She died in 2003.

NATO ALPHABET

Thanks to its deemed familiarity throughout the world, **'whiskey'** (American/Irish spelling) was selected to represent the letter 'W' in the international phonetic alphabet much used by those in The Services and Air Traffic Control.

NECK AND NECK *

Observant visitors to distilleries will have noticed that the swan-like neck on the copper stills invariably points downwards. The more perceptive will have realised that some necks in fact veer towards the horizontal. Few will have noticed, however, that there are only one or two necks in all of Scotland's malt distilleries which are inclined upwards (this aids the **reflux** process), **Laphroaig** on Islay being one of them (source: Forsyths Group, Rothes).

* **Author's note:** for necking enthusiasts there is a wonderful poster available on www.whiskyposter.de

NEW BLENDS
There are hundreds of different brands of blended Scotch Whisky. Add to this the equally numerous brands of other blended whiskies in the world which cannot be called 'scotch whisky' and one begins to wonder why anyone might wish to create yet another blend. The answer is **commerce**. It is this very aspect which drove the founding fathers of Scotch Whisky in the mid and late 20th century and which has propelled the industry throughout the 20th century. In this respect, the role of the **Master Blender** is crucial to success. Nowadays, the initial impetus for a new blend is likely to stem from the marketing team. A new market penetration, changing market tastes, a necessity to compete head-to-head, a major event or anniversary requiring recognition – these might be just some of the reasons precipitating a drive to produce a new and successful blend.

The Master Blender's **brief** is more than likely very short and to the point – including terms such as light, heavy, colour, aromatic, aperitif, age of target drinkers, etc. He or she will be given the parameters within which the new product will require to operate, including consumer market and annual volumes. From this information and, additionally, the massive databank of certain major companies, the blending team set to work.

Critically, their task is also to determine if the company has access to the requisite stock for the initial and subsequent production runs. As Colin Scott, Master Blender at **Chivas**

[Bold text within paragraphs refers to sub-headings in the Index]

Brothers emphasises, there is little point in making a superb blend if the means to continual supply may not persist, unless it is for a special limited product.

Also: Aged Inventory; Blending

NEW MAKE SPIRIT

Aptly named, the Gaelic word for this astonishingly clear liquid is **clearic**. It is this liquid which, placed into the barrels for maturing, eventually becomes whisky (source: Lagavulin distillery visit).

Also: White Whisky

NEW PRODUCTS

In one respect, the whisky industry is little different from other industries; the concept for a new product will be driven by the need to generate profits. But the time-lag from conception to consumption for some major new whisky products can be considerable. Certain producers have to make crucial decisions far in advance – anything from a minimum of 10 years to upwards of 20 years. At the higher end of the spectrum this may be governed by any **age statement** which will appear on the whisky label.

The **Glenmorangie wood finish** series* is a case in point. The finishing technique was developed by them in the late 1980's. From this finding, they then went on to perfect their 'wood finish' in **Port**, **Madeira** and **Sherry** casks.

Glenmorangie's core products – their 10, 15 and 18 year old single malts together with their Port, Madeira and Sherry finished single malts pass through a process of evolution spanning some 20 + years (in the instance of the 18 year old).

Also: Foresight; Sales Projections; Sign Here!

* These now comprise 18% of Glenmorangie's total sales by volume (source: Glenmorangie plc).

NICHE MARKETS

The power of marketing and niche markets was recognised by

a number of the pioneers of today's whisky industry. When John Grant acquired the Speyside Farm in 1865 and purchased the adjacent **Glenfarclas** Distillery, he quickly established a staging post for the **drovers** taking their animals to market. However, this pales into insignificance when seen against the success of **Glenfiddich**, which pioneered the niche category of malts in the mid 1960s.

Also: Sign Here!

[Bold text within paragraphs refers to sub-headings in the Index]

O

OAK

In 1988 the legal definition of whisky was changed to specify that the spirit had to be matured in **oak casks**. Over the years, whisky had been stored in various types of wooden casks, but it was realised that oak gave a better end product. It was also clear that **second-hand casks** (those previously used for storing other drinks such as port, sherry, bourbon) produced a more flavoured whisky than new casks. Oak contains **hemicellulose** which gives sweetness and colour. The **oak wood** also contains **lignin** which produces **vanillin** and **coconut flavours**. However, it is only by the previous application of heat to the inside surface of the oak cask – **charring** or in the case of a lighter application of heat, **toasting** – that the oak wood can be induced to give up these flavours to the new make spirit maturing inside the oak cask.

Also: Charring; Scotch Whisky Act 1988; Wood Sourcing

OAK CASKS

1946 was a pivotal year and one which witnessed a substitution of **European oak** for **American oak** casks. This period was witnessing a boom in whisky exports as Britain strove to pay off its massive debts incurred during the Second World War. At the same time, the United States was consuming ever more bourbon, with the abolition of Prohibition. By law, a bourbon cask could only be used once in the maturation of Bourbon Whiskey. The shiploads of whisky exports from Scotland, therefore found a ready return load and this in turn helped the Exchequer. This change led to the diminution of **sherry** flavoured (European) oak casks in favour of (American) **bourbon** oak with its higher **vanillin** content and reduced **tannins**.

OCTOMORE

The malted barley used to make this new single malt, from **Bruichladdich** Distillery on Islay (first distilled in 2003) has a **phenol content** of 80.5 parts per million. It is the most highly peated single malt whisky in the world (source: distillery visit).

Also: Phenols

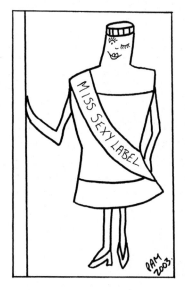

OFF THE SHELF

New world wine makers have frequently considered their unusual labels to be a useful means of shifting stock from the supermarket shelves. In their autumn 2001 'Review', **Glenfarclas** reported a 29% increase in UK sales of their 10 year old, when packaged in a visually striking '**Flower of Scotland**' gift tin (source: J. & G. Grant).

Also: Plastic; Tube

OLDEST (Independent)

Springbank is the oldest independent distillery to remain under the direct control of the founder's family.

OLDEST (Licensed)

Bushmills Distillery in Northern Ireland is sometimes cited as the oldest licensed malt distillery in the United Kingdom. However as was pointed out by Alex Kraaijeveld, whisky writer and biologist, there is no evidence Bushmills existed before 1784. What happened in 1608 is that a licence to distil was granted for the area around Bushmills, not to a specific distillery.

[Bold text within paragraphs refers to sub-headings in the Index]

OWNERSHIP OF WORKING MALT WHISKY DISTILLERIES IN SCOTLAND*

Allied Domecq (Ardmore; Glenburgie; Glendronach; Glentauchers; Laphroaig; Miltonduff; Scapa; Strathclyde *(grain)*; Tormore)

NOTE: Imperial is mothballed

Angus Dundee plc (Glencadam; Tomintoul)

Armstrong, Raymond (Bladnoch)

Bacardi (Aberfeldy; Aultmore; Craigellachie; Macduff; Royal Brackla)

Benriach Distillery Company Ltd (Benriach)

Bruichladdich Whisky Company Ltd (Bruichladdich)

CL World Brands (Deanston; Tobermory; Bunnahabhain)

Diageo (Auchroisk; Benrinnes; Blair Atholl; Cameronbridge *(grain)*; Caol Ila; Cardhu; Clynelish; Cragganmore; Dailuaine; Dalwhinnie; Dufftown; Glendullan; Glen Elgin; Glenkinchie; Glenlossie; Glen Ord; Glen Spey; Inchgower; Knockando; Lagavulin; Linkwood; Mannochmore; Mortlach; North British *(grain)* - jointly owned with Edrington; Oban; Port Dundas *(grain)*; Royal Lochnagar; Strathmill; Talisker; Teaninich)

NOTE: Pittyvaich is mothballed

The Edrington Group Ltd (Glenrothes; Glenturret; Highland Park; North British *(grain)* - jointly owned with Diageo; The Macallan; Tamdhu)

Glenmorangie plc (Ardbeg; Glenmorangie; Glen Moray)

Gordon & MacPhail Ltd (Benromach)

Ian MacLeod & Co. Ltd (Glengoyne)

Isle of Arran Distillers Ltd (Arran)

J & A Mitchell & Co. Ltd (Springbank; Glengyle)

J. & G. Grant Ltd (Glenfarclas)

Loch Lomond Distillery Co. Ltd (Glen Scotia; Loch Lomond (malt and grain))

Nikka (Ben Nevis)

Pacific Spirits UK (Balblair; Balmenach; Knockdhu; Old Pulteney; Speyburn)

Pernod Ricard (Aberlour; Glenallachie; Glen Grant; The Glenlivet; Longmorn; Strathisla)
NOTE: Braeval (originally Braes of Glenlivet); Allt-a-Bhainne; Caperdonich and Glen Keith are mothballed
Signatory Vintage Scotch Whisky Company Ltd (Edradour)
Speyside Distillers Company Ltd (Speyside)
Suntory (Auchentoshan; Bowmore; Glengarioch)
Takara - Shuzo - Marubeni (Tomatin)
Tullibardine Consortium (Tullibardine) **
Whyte & Mackay Ltd (Dalmore; Fettercairn; Invergordon *(grain)*; Isle of Jura)
NOTE: Tamnavulin is mothballed
Wm Grant & Sons (Girvan *(grain)*; Glenfiddich; Kininvie; The Balvenie)

* by parent company and distillery name – believed correct at time of writing
** at time of writing, production is restarting, in conjunction with 'tourist retail park'.

OZARK MOUNTAINS

The long haul to a perfect dram begins deep in the heart of **Missouri** in the United States. Here, a proportion of the casks used by **Glenmorangie plc** is made from specially selected American white oak grown in The Ozark Mountains. Years of research* convinced the company that, if they wanted to produce perfect whisky, they had to have access to the best wood. This meant having control over the process by which their casks were produced and handled.

Glenmorangie established that, in this part of the United States, the poorer, dry soils produce a **slow growing oak**. The result is a wood with relatively open pores. The maturing whisky can penetrate the wood more easily and derive more 'goodness' (more **vanilla** and other **aromatics**) during maturation. The wood is then seasoned slowly in the open air for two years, as opposed to being rushed through as it is in the

[Bold text within paragraphs refers to sub-headings in the Index]

more modern and speedier kiln dried process. Glenmorangie plc has its own local representatives (**The Blue Grass Cooperage**) to select and monitor the oak from forest to distillery. After a life of 4 years spent filled with **bourbon**, the empty oak casks are imported 'whole' (complete with bung in place to retain essential aromas) filled with Glenmorangie at Tain and placed in their warehouses for maturation.

Also: Wood Sourcing; New Products

* Extensive research was undertaken by Glenmorangie to understand how wood and whisky were reacting. As their current Distillery Manager put it, the objective was 'to find the ideal designer cask'.

P

'PAGODA'

This distinctive style of roof was invented in the 1880s, to improve the flow of air through the kiln. The inventor, **Charles Chree Doig**, (1855 – 1918) Civil Engineer and Architect, Elgin* was responsible for the design and construction of numerous distilleries in Scotland. The first distillery to adopt this style of roof was **Dailuaine**.

Also: Balblair Distillery

* thanks to Graeme Wilson, Local Heritage Officer, The Library, Elgin.

PALLETS

One of industry's great leaps forward in the 20th century was the introduction of the humble pallet – a wooden platform of varying size on which all manner of goods could be lifted and repositioned. The traditional nature of the whisky industry meant that it was perhaps slower than most to take full advantage of this aid to industry, not least because their traditional single storey **dunnage warehouse** with the whisky casks stacked three-high did not offer sufficient space for the fork-lift truck, the essential device for moving pallets. However, with the establishment of massive warehousing complexes (such as **Mulben**, near Keith) in the early 1970s it was only going to be a matter of time before accountants, pressing for ever-greater savings, realised that they could increase warehousing storage, dramatically, if the **whisky casks** were stored upright and in units of (say) six per pallet. Broadly speaking, for the same volume of warehouse space, maturing the whisky in this manner increases the volume stored by some 30%. Given the cost of land and the potential difficulties of obtaining **Planning Permission** in certain rural

[Bold text within paragraphs refers to sub-headings in the Index]

locations, this is not an insignificant breakthrough. For the traditionalists, however, there is always the concern that insufficient air may be circulating around more tightly packed pallets of maturing whisky.

Also: Stack 'em High; Warehousing

PASSWORD

Customs and Excise officers have the right to be issued with their own password to obtain 'read only' access to distillery **electronic accounting systems** (source: Customs and Excise Notice 197, 2002, section 36).

Also: In And Out

PATRONAGE

There are only two distilleries which incorporate the word 'royal'. These are **Royal Brackla** granted in 1835 and **Royal Lochnagar** granted in 1848. Glenury Distillery at Stonehaven – now demolished – also carried the term, as in **Glenury Royal**.

PEAT

The use of peat **caff** (powdered peat) instead of the more usual lumps of peat, can significantly reduce the consumption of peat used in the kiln drying process at the malting barns. It is, however, something of an art to be able to keep the **peat fire** 'in' and not smother it. Damp peats can also slow the burn, but getting the correct mix of damp to dry can prove even more challenging (source: distillery visits).

Also: Kiln Drying

PEAT INFLUENCE

It would have come as a bit of a shock to the earlier generations of household distillers, drying their **malted barley** over the peat fire, to know (in the words of G.H. Palmer*) that **phenolic substances** such as **isomeric cresols**, **guaiacol** and **xylenols** are deposited on the malt during the **peating process**. It is these

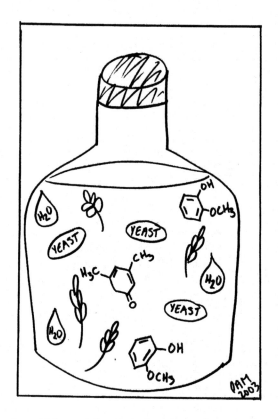

deposits which contribute to the **smoky aroma** of certain whiskies.

Also: Efficiency versus Tradition; Octomore

* Professor of Cereal Science, Heriot Watt University; in his illuminating paper, 'A Wee Dram of Whisky' (Liquid Foods International; January, 1999).

PECKING ORDER

Before the introduction of **complimentary bottles** being issued to staff in the mid to late '80s, there was a code of practice which resulted in the Manager, Cooper and Exciseman

[Bold text within paragraphs refers to sub-headings in the Index]

enjoying quality whisky from the premises. By contrast, the Brewer had to make do with **new make spirit** and the other staff with what they could purloin. The **clocking on dram** and the **clocking off dram** were a regular feature of distillery life (source: Exciseman Anonymous).

Also: Dramming; Tiring Work

PERSONALISED NUMBER PLATE

Where can you spot 'DAL 12 Y' on the lorry used to transport the casks around the distillery site?

Also: Answer

PHENOLS

One of the characteristics that distilleries aim for in their **malted barley** is a certain **phenol content**. This is specified as ppm (parts per million). Some instructive examples obtained during distillery visits are: **Ardbeg** 56.2 ppm; **Lagavulin** 30-40ppm; **Isle of Jura** 1-2 ppm; **Springbank** 15ppm (by contrast, their **Longrow** single malt uses malted barley with a phenol content of 45-50ppm). Expressed in layman's terminology, these figures reflect the higher (50) and lower (15) **influence of peat** during the malting process.

The malted barley used in a typical Speyside malt, such as **Cragganmore**, has perhaps twenty times less exposure to peat smoke than that used to make an Islay malt, such as **Lagavulin** (latter's distillery leaflet). By contrast, a number of distilleries (for example **Balblair**) are producing single malt whiskies with zero phenol content. This is because they prefer to use malted barley which has not been subjected to any peat smoke.

To achieve the specified ppm laid down by the customer the **Maltings** will mix the malted barley until arriving at the necessary figure. Ratings around the 10 – 15 ppm tend to be more difficult to guage than at the opposite extremes of 2ppm or 40 ppm (source: site visits).

Also: Kiln Drying; Octomore

PHENOLS AND PROCESSING

In general, the higher the **phenol content** of the **malted barley**, the longer is the **fermentation period** required to convert the necessary **sugars**. Every distillery is different but, as a general yardstick, you may find an average of approximately two days fermentation, increasing to approximately three days, for those distilleries using malted barley with a higher phenol content (source: visit to Ardbeg Distillery).

Also: Important Stages

PHILOSOPHER

Always a man for subtle observation, **Tommy Dewar** opined that 'A philosopher is a man who can look at an empty glass with a smile' (source: John Dewar & Sons Ltd).

Also: Aberfeldy Distillery

PIECEWORK

The coopers at **Speyside Cooperage** in **Craigellachie** are paid according to the amount of work they do. In addition, the coopers each work on a particular project from start to finish, thus aiding quality control (source: site visit).

PIPE DREAMS

During the installation of a fire prevention sprinkler system in a whisky warehouse it became apparent that cases of whisky were being opened and pilfered. By chance, it was noticed that one particular person was carrying a length of pipe out of the area and shortly afterwards returning with it. On the outward journey only, the ends of the pipe were stuffed with canvas, so keeping the bottles secure inside (source: Exciseman Anonymous).

Also: Domestic Disruptions

PLAIN BRITISH SPIRIT

This is the term given to the liquid (also known as **new make spirit**) prior to it having matured for the minimum three years

[Bold text within paragraphs refers to sub-headings in the Index]

in **oak casks**, thereafter which it can legally be termed Scotch Whisky. It is in effect the **middle cut** passing through the **Spirit Still** (also called the **Low Wines and Feints Still**) to the **Spirit Receiver** and thence to the **Filling Store**, where it is put into oak casks for maturation (source: Historic Scotland, Dallas Dhu Distillery).

Also:New Make Spirit

PLASTIC
It was only a matter of time before the security conscious airports started to introduce plastic bottles. For example, Gordons London Dry (Gin), Three Barrels (Brandy) and Teachers Highland Cream Scotch Whisky are now being sold in litre bottles at Duty Free, Gatwick Airport.

Also: Off The Shelf; Tube

PLAYERS AND MANAGERS
Analogies in the whisky industry abound, but it is useful to think of the great football managers Jock Stein or Alex Ferguson, in the role of Master Blender. Colin Scott, Master Blender at **Chivas Brothers,** likens the skill of a good blender to one who understands his 'players'. He sees his available stock of **single malts** and **single grain whiskies** as the material upon which he can call to produce the perfectly formed 'team'. He knows which ones are critical to success and, furthermore, understands how others in his pool can be called upon to influence the team's performance when one of the players is unable to function fully, for whatever reason. The average mix of 20 – 30 whiskies, which comprise a typical **Scotch Blend**, can be seen in the same light. For the layman, it is a useful introduction (albeit a gross over-simplification) to the skill of the Blender.

Also: Aged Inventory; Blending: Impact; Master Blender

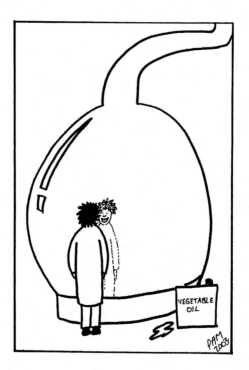

POLISHING

Some old distillery hands know that rubbing the exterior of the copper stills with **vegetable oil** is the best way to retain the highly burnished polish.

> With a dram of my Craigellachie
> A snifter of your Glenallachie,
> I'll polish my dome,
> 'Till the cows come home
> Then sample a wee Glendronach-y

POMPEYING

One can only guess at the origin of the term* – as mentioned by Kenneth Kilby in his book 'The Cooper and His Trade' (Linden Publishing, 1989) – used to signify the **charring**

[Bold text within paragraphs refers to sub-headings in the Index]

process for the insides of wine, spirit and stout casks. For each of the trades, he remarks that the common objective was to assist maturation and provide distinctive flavours.

Also: Charring; Toasting

* as in Campania, Italy or Portsmouth, England.

POPULARITY

It was only after **Andrew Usher** pioneered the practice of **blending** in the early 1860's (in Edinburgh) that a taste for Scotch Whisky spread first to England and then throughout the world. Up until then, the whisky product (being as it was a single malt whisky) was inclined to be too strongly flavoured for those in sedentary occupations and warm climates (source: The Scotch Whisky Association).

Also: Bagpipes; Blending; Dewarisms

PRICES

At a time when an average bottle of single malt was costing approximately £18 – £24, the record price of £25,877 pounds sterling, was being paid to purchase a bottle of 62 year old **Dalmore single malt** on 4th December, 2002 at a special auction in Glasgow.

PRINCE CHARLES

HRH The Prince of Wales signed the first cask stored in the warehouse at the official re-opening of **Benromach** Distillery in 1998 (source: Gordon & MacPhail).

PRODUCTION PROCESS

Springbank Distillery is the only distillery to carry out the full production process from traditional **floor maltings** to bottling on site (source: Springbank Distillers Ltd).

PRONUNCIATION

Ask for a 'boon-a hav-in' (**Bunnahabhain**) a very lightly peated Islay malt but if you prefer a really strong, peat flavoured malt ask for a 'laugh-roy-g' (**Laphroaig**). An in-between-one might be a 'brook-laddie' (**Bruichladdich**) or a 'cul-ee-la' (**Caol Ila**). The French will of course invariably ask for a 'glen-feed-eesh', whilst even the Scots can forget that the correct way to ask for a **Glenmorangie** is to think of that 'orangey' flavour (which it doesn't have). Never ask for an 'och-roysk' (as in a throat-clearing 'loch', not 'lok') because the owners of the **Auchroisk** Distillery felt that potential customers could only pronounce (**The**) **Singleton**. Finally if your courage or memory fails you, just point.

Also: (the distilleries at) Auchroisk; Bruichladdich;
Bunnahabhain; Caol Ila; Laphroaig

PROOF STRENGTH

To convert from American **degree proof**, to British and European percentage **alcohol by volume** (abv) divide the American figure by two.

Also: Gunpowder

PROVIDED HOUSE

1983 was a pivotal year for the distillers and Customs & Excise. In subsequent years the former took over the responsibility for **revenue operations** and the latter adopted the role of supervisor. Prior to that date the **Excise** had an office at each distillery and such were the hours of possible work, for example due to necessary repairs outwith the 9 – 5 office routine, that the distiller was legally bound to provide a house at a nominal rent. The 'provided house' as it was termed, bound the excise officer into the community and indeed there was a time when the position was held in almost equal esteem to that of the local banker, minister and headmaster. On **Speyside**, the last of the provided houses (at **Tamnavulin** and **Glenlivet** distilleries) was handed back in 1985.

Also: Communities

PUGGIE

The affectionate name given to the beautifully restored 1939

[Bold text within paragraphs refers to sub-headings in the Index]

steam locomotive which sits outside **Aberfeldy** Distillery (source: John Dewar & Sons Ltd). The word is cited in The Oxford English Dictionary as being a small locomotive used for shunting and was also the name of the steam engine which ran on the branch line from **Cromdale** to **Balmenach** Distillery at the end of the 1930's and which is now in the care of The **Strathspey Railway Company** (source: Miss S.R. Birnie, Grantown-on-Spey).

Also: Ballindalloch

PUNCHEON
A whisky butt also holds the same quantity of liquid as this cask: 500 litres.

Also: Capacities

PURE MALT
To the layman the closest thing to a whisky oxymoron must be a pure malt*. Passing through Duty Free at Prague International Airport in December, 2003, the author's attention was drawn to 8 year old **Blairmhor Pure Malt.** 'Distilled and matured by **R.Carmichael & Sons Ltd** Airdrie (it is) created from a finely balanced selection of malts'. Additional reading of the label revealed that Blairmhor 'contains 20 single malts, the majority of them are from The Highland and Speyside Regions of Scotland'. A competing brand on a nearby shelf – 12 year old **Cardhu Pure Malt** ** produced by **Diageo** – informed the reader that this 'combines complementary single malts to create a pure Speyside Malt'. A comparison of prices showed the Cardhu Pure Malt to be approximately three times more expensive than the Blairmhor Pure Malt.

Also: Vatted Malt

* The Scotch Whisky Association is in the process of setting out **definitions** to clarify the meaning of **single malt** and the **variants** created from mixing them together.

** Diageo has since withdrawn Cardhu Pure Malt from the market.

PURGATORY

In the late 1980s the author had the good fortune to be invited by the Laird of Ulva to share his favourite 'dram' for the evening: tumblers of 25 year old **The Macallan** were duly served.

PURIFIERS

Distillers have long recognised that the **heavier vapours,** created during the distillation process in the **copper stills,** are contributory to a distinctive and dominant whisky. For the average palate, these can be over-bearing and, so it was, that one of the earlier pioneers of innovative thinking found a solution to suit his ideal whisky. '**The Major**', who was proprietor at **Glen Grant** from 1872 until his death in 1931, solved the problem by placing a purifier on the **lyne* arm** of the pot still. Resembling a small copper tub, this ingenious device lets the **lighter vapours** pass through to the **condenser,** but condenses the heavier vapours and returns the latter back into the still for re-distillation (source: distillery visit and booklet 'Glen Grant Distillery and Woodland Garden').

Also: Sweetness; Shapes And Sizes

* it may also be written 'lye', as in the quoted source.

[Bold text within paragraphs refers to sub-headings in the Index]

Q

QUANTITIES OF GRAIN

An average size **malt whisky distillery** will use approximately 5,000 tonnes of malted barley per annum. By contrast the much larger **grain whisky distilleries**, such as **Invergordon**, will use approximately 80,000 tonnes of grain (in Scotland the specific grain used is determined by market prices and consequently this is generally wheat, although one distillery is still using maize). In addition some 7,000 tonnes of **malted barley** will also be used by a grain distillery, such as Invergordon, to convert the **starch** in the grain into **sugar** (source: distillery visits).

Also: Wheat

QUEEN MARY 2

Somewhat surprisingly, if you are looking for a dram of their own exclusive label whilst enjoying your luxury cruise, your only option is to purchase a litre bottle from the Duty Free Shop aboard ship. The liner's Bar List sports the usual regular blends and malts – a high proportion being **Diageo** brands – but not the Queen Mary 2 (source: Don Greig, Inverness).

QUEEN'S SILVER JUBILEE

Tucked away at the foot of The **Cromdale Hills** is the caption to crown all. Carefully engraved by **Abercrombie's** coppersmiths on one of Balmenach's stills, you will find the statement that it was transported to London to represent Scotland's whisky industry at the **Jubilee Celebrations** of **Her Majesty Queen Elizabeth**. Why **Balmenach**? Quite simply the order for their still and its completion (before installation) coincided with that momentous date (source: distillery visit).

Also: Inflation

QUICK THINKING

When the Excise raided Great Great Grannie **MacSporran's** house near Machrihanish in search of **illicit whisky**, the intrepid lady spread her ample skirts around her stool and the cask was never found (source: Miss F. Petrie, Kippen).

[Bold text within paragraphs refers to sub-headings in the Index]

R

RACKING
The term used for the transferring of the contents of one cask to another in order to deal with excessive **leakage** or to improve the **maturation** process (for example, the Dalmore 62 year old which was recently auctioned at £25,877 for a bottle, was racked four times in order to obtain the desired style*). Racking can also refer to the general process of filling a cask.

Also: First

* source: Whisky Magazine, 'Desert Island Drams' by Richard Jones; May, 2003.

RAILWAY DRAMS
The railway staff sometimes obtained whisky from leaking barrels with potentially dire consequences. The railway clerk at **Ballindalloch Station** not only had to deal with passengers and parcels, but *in extremis* was required to act as signalman and pass a train along the single track line. This involved accepting it from the previous signal box and guiding it safely through the station and passing it on to the next section. **The Boozer**, as it was affectionately termed, was due to pass through the station on its regular Saturday evening run from Craigellachie to Boat of Garten. The clerk had been aware that the signalman was a bit under the weather that evening and had come back to the station before the train was due. The signalman was stretched out on the floor behind the levers and fast asleep (source: Bill Murray, Fair Isle and formerly employed at Ballindalloch Station).

Also: Ballindalloch; Domestic Disruptions
The signalman worked on the railway
And was always contented on pay day
With his flask of Cardhu,
Or was it really Tamdhu?
He forgot all about trains on their way

RATIONING

After the **Second World War** whisky remained on ration in Britain until 1959 (source: The Making of Scotch Whisky; Michael Moss & John Hume, James & James, 1981).

RAW MATERIAL COSTS

To produce **new make spirit** in a malt distillery ready for maturing in oak casks (which after three years can then be termed Scotch Whisky) the major raw materials required are: **water, malted barley, yeast** and **energy**. Given that 70 – 75 per cent of the cost of producing new make spirit is the malted barley, it is hardly surprising that distilleries are constantly trying to maximise the yield of **alcohol** per tonne of malted barley.

To spread the risk of the malted barley not being up to standard, most distilleries will purchase their malted barley from a number of maltings. The distillery will be sent a sample a few days in advance in order that both parties can be satisfied as to specification. On arrival of the bulk delivery, a sample will be taken and sent to the distiller's **laboratories** for final analysis and checking. Should the quality of the subsequent new make spirit be called into question, then part of the sample will be sent to the **maltings** and part to an independent test source for final adjudication – the maltings is also likely to have held back and 'filed' a sample from the bulk delivery (source: distillery visits).

Also: Barley; Malting The Barley; Yield

READY FOR THE ROAD

The Distillery Manager, knowing that the young Exciseman was being transferred to a post in England, enquired if he was 'well shod' for the journey, and presented two bottles of vintage product to ease the parting from Speyside (source: Exciseman Anonymous).

Also: Communities

[Bold text within paragraphs refers to sub-headings in the Index]

RECIPROCALS

With most blends containing anything from 20 – 50 different malts (plus one or two grain whiskies) the reader might surmise that there must be a lot of whisky on the move in Scotland, before the bottle is finally capped and crated. The term for the **bulk exchange** of malt whisky and grain whisky is 'reciprocals' and it is characterised by the gentlemanly code, whereby no money changes hands. Resembling **bartering**, this is an activity unique to the whisky industry and one in which diligent **book-keeping** is essential. The basic unit of exchange is 2 litres of single grain whisky = 1 litre of single malt whisky. From this base line are added (or deducted) percentages for factors such as, for example, Islay malts are considered to be approximately 30 per cent more expensive than most mainland malts. Then there are percentage allowances for age of maturity and for specific distillery names, which may be deemed premium makes. Rigorous book-keeping is necessary to keep the accountants happy and, meanwhile, the blenders are able to get on with their task (source: distillery visits).

Also: Commodity Trading; Devil In The Detail

RECORD KEEPING

It was in the early 1980s that the onus for calculating the **excise duty** due to the Government moved from the Exciseman, frequently located at each distillery, to the Distillery Manager. Whereas the **Excise** might have used his judgement to be flexible in his approach to keeping records, the new system of self-policing has probably created a much more efficient tax collecting system for the Government. Nowadays, the distillery manager must justify his stock monthly, to within 0.5 litres – no mean task (source: Ardbeg Distillery visit).

Also: Balancing The Books

RECYCLING

It is instructive to note that the source of all copper used in the making of the copper stills and other distillery equipment is the one remaining (copper) **rolling mill** in the UK. That particular plant sources 75% of its raw material from scrap copper (source: Forsyths Group, Rothes).

Also: Copper

REGIONAL PRODUCTION

Lowland malts are generally light in colour and typically have a dry finish. They are located south of a line from **Montrose** to **Dumbarton** (roughly following the geological '**Highland Boundary Fault**'). They do not include the distilleries of Arran and Campbeltown.

The latter are included in the **Highland** malts. This encompasses the area north of the above mentioned line. There are many variations in style from within this large area and indeed some purists will sub-divide the Highland area into: Northern, Eastern, Southern and Western Highland malts and of course the **Campbeltown** malts. The latter are considered by many to rank as a clearly defined category alongside the other principal four: Lowland, Highland, Islay and Speyside.

However, there are two universally agreed Highland sub-divisions and these are: **Islay** malts and **Speyside** malts. The latter group contains almost as many distilleries in this geographically small area, as all the other areas in Scotland combined (see Sketch Map of Distillery Locations).

Also: Highland Boundary Fault

RENEWABLE ENERGY

Long before the 'accountants' were looking for energy saving measures, staff at distilleries prone to severe frosts – such as **Balmenach** – would store the **yeast** in the Tun Room. Here the heat from the **fermentation** in the **Wash Backs** helped to retain the vitality of the yeast until it was ready for use (source: distillery visit).

Also: Fermentation

[Bold text within paragraphs refers to sub-headings in the Index]

RETIRED?

'No, just changing jobs' might have been the reply offered by 'Mr Whisky' * – Iain Henderson – when he retired as Distillery Manager at **Laphroaig** and was snapped up by **Edradour**.

   * some of his younger (female) colleagues on Islay refer to this illustrious gentleman in such affectionate terms.

REVENUE VALUE

Much is made of the high **tax** (duty) paid by distillers and the public alike on a bottle of whisky. For the record, and at the time of writing, **duty** is currently charged by Customs and **Excise** at £19.56 per litre of **alcohol** (100 per cent abv). For the Government, the 'Revenue Value' of a distillery is the hypothetical figure calculated on the total duty that would be paid if all **new make spirit** was taxed. Fortunately for the distillery companies – given that the average medium-sized malt distillery is producing some 2 million litres of alcohol per year – the duty is paid ONLY on the volume which is released to the domestic market. With some 90 – 95 per cent of production exported, revenue raised comes down to manageable proportions (source: Exciseman Anonymous).

Also: Balancing The Books; Islay and Jura; Tax

RIVETED

In the years following the **Second World War**, the industry was transfixed by the prospect that the traditional **riveted copper stills** were in the process of being replaced by stills with **welded seams**. Indeed, the then owner of Glenlivet Distillery was of the opinion that 'A still without rivets is like a lady without clothes'. The welding skills brought back by the demobbed servicemen (including no less a man than **Ernest 'Toot' Forsyth**) hastened this transformation, much to the consternation of the old and very traditional owners (source: Forsyths Group, Rothes).

Also: Welding

ROOTS

Lineage counts for a lot as Glenfarclas, Glenfiddich and Springbank would testify, which is why Balmenach is proud to point out that the current Distillery Manager's wife is the great great grand-daughter of the original owners!

ROTHES

In its heyday, **Campbeltown** would have been the whisky town of its time with upwards of 20 distilleries in the closing decades of the 19th century. Today such concentrations of whisky production and ancillary trades are hard to find anywhere in Scotland. Rothes has five distilleries: **'The Gibbet'**, **'Glennies'**, **'Caper'**, **'The Heilan'** and **'Gilbeys'***. It also has a Dark Grains Plant and the renowned coppersmiths, **Forsyths**. All are clustered around its main street. Rothes is perhaps the closest one will find to a whisky town, although **Dufftown** continues to have six working distilleries, but its ancillary trades are reduced to the services of one vat builder, **Joseph Brown**.

Also: Milestones

* the affectionate local names for: **Speyburn** (the location of the device), **Glen Grant**, **Caperdonich** (mothballed), **Glenrothes** and **Glen Spey** (previously owned by W & A Gilbey Ltd).

ROYAL BRACKLA DISTILLERY

The product from this distillery near Nairn, was the first to be granted a **Royal Warrant**, by King William 1V in 1835 (source: John Dewar & Sons Ltd).

Also:Illicit Stills; Siskin; Usher Hall

ROYAL LOCHNAGAR DISTILLERY

In 1976 and subsequently for a period of some ten years, the then owners, **Distillers Company Ltd** (DCL), removed the **Royal Patronage**. This extraordinary action arose from the fact that in a speech to the Pot-Still Malt Distillers' Association in Elgin, **The Duke of Edinburgh** criticised the distillery 'for polluting the grounds of **Balmoral**'. DCL's Chief Accountant

[Bold text within paragraphs refers to sub-headings in the Index]

was incensed and insisted that the 'Royal' be removed from all packaging and signage. This was eventually reinstated in the mid-1980s, with the Royal Household's permission (source: Charles MacLean in The Scotch Malt Whisky Society's issue 97; May, 2002).

RYE WHISKEY

Rye Whiskey is produced both in the **United States** and **Canada**, but the name has no geographical significance. In the United States, Rye Whiskey, by definition, must be produced from a grain mash of which not less than 51 per cent is **rye grain**. In Canada (where whisky is spelt without an 'e') there is no similar restriction.

The relevant **Canadian Regulation** states:

'**Canadian Whisky** (Canadian Rye Whisky, Rye Whisky) shall be whisky distilled in Canada, and shall possess the aroma, taste and character generally attributed to Canadian Whisky.'

Canadian Whisky is in fact often referred to simply as Rye Whisky or **Rye** (source: The Scotch Whisky Association).

Also: Bourbon Whiskey

S

SACCHAROMETER
This is a type of **hydrometer** used to measure the amount of dissolved sugar in the **wort** or **wash**.

SACRIFICIAL COPPER
Sacrificial copper is quite simply fine copper turnings through which part of the product stream is passed to dissolve trace amounts of the metal. Copper is considered an essential component in the making of whisky. One cannot make good whisky without the contribution that is derived from copper during the **distillation process**. In the malt whisky distilleries this is obtained through **chemical interaction** with the traditional (copper) **pot stills**. However, in some **grain whisky distilleries**, where the stills are now more commonly made from **stainless steel**, sacrificial copper will be used. Some grain distilleries will have structural copper in their stills and this is eroded, so releasing the copper. In addition it is not unusual for the **rectifier** (part of the grain distillery's **Patent** or **Coffey still**) to have some copper plates through which the hot vapours rise (source: distillery visits).

Also: Copper

SALAD CREAM
Empty salad cream bottles made excellent '**dunkers**', fitting neatly through the bung hole in the whisky cask, when employees wanted to share some with the 'angel' (source: Exciseman Anonymous).

Also: Frisky

SALES PROJECTIONS
The **Scotch Whisky Industry** has the conundrum of trying to

[Bold text within paragraphs refers to sub-headings in the Index]

predict **demand** for the product it is making today, but which (by legal definition) cannot be ready for at least three years and often (depending upon the final product) some ten years or more ahead. In 2002, **stocks** of mature and maturing whisky were sufficient to cover projected sales for the next nine years (source: The Scotch Whisky Association).

Also: Foresight; New Products

SALMON

Craigellachie Distillery has now adopted the Spey salmon as a symbol for its whisky, to reflect the energy and determination of the distillery's founder, Peter J Mackie – more fondly known as '**Restless Peter**' (source: John Dewar & Sons Ltd).

Also: Fly Fishing; Shipping

SAMPLING

Whereas there is ample anecdotal evidence of distillery employees having had recourse to the occasional sample in their day-to-day routine, current regulations imposed by HM Customs and Excise (since the abolition of the **Excise** being based at each distillery) have resulted in more rigid controls. Nowadays, each distillery is responsible for keeping scrupulous records – for example, all samples must be properly accounted for and any unused samples destroyed, with a record kept of their disposal (all as specified in HM Customs and Excise's **Notice 39**, 2002, clause 6.8).

Also: In and Out

SCOTCH WHISKY ACT 1988

As defined in this Act, Scotch Whisky is whisky which has been produced at a distillery in Scotland from water and malted barley. It must be matured in an excise **warehouse** in Scotland in **oak casks** of a capacity not exceeding 700 litres and the period of that **maturation** must not be less than three years. The said whisky must have an **alcohol strength** between 40 and 94.8 per cent by volume. Full details are laid down in the

Act and a clear summary is contained in the excellent booklet published by The Scotch Whisky Association: 'Scotch Whisky Questions & Answers'.

Also: Glen Turner; Oak

SCOTCH WHISKY RESEARCH INSTITUTE
Located on the **Heriot Watt University** Campus in Edinburgh, this is a membership organisation for the **Whisky Industry** and much of the information and data held is confidential to its members.

SCOTS OR SCOTCH?
Most whisky labels refer to the drink as Scotch. One of the exceptions to the rule is the blend, **Cutty Sark**. Their label identifies it as 'original Scots Whisky' with the line below stating that it is '**Blended Scots Whisky** from Scotland's Famous Distilleries' (source: Cutty Sark label).

Also: Cutty Sark

SCOTTISH TECHNOLOGY
Japanese whisky manufacturers have been to the fore in using the skills, knowledge and products of Scotland's whisky industry to enhance their own manufacturing process. Of the foreign manufacturers of whisky ranging across **Australia, Canada, Czech Republic*, India, Pakistan** and the **United States**, it is the Japanese products which are consistently superior and closest to the Scottish product.

Also: Craftsmanship

* The **Likerka Dolany Distillery** was put into liquidation in 2003 (source: site visit).

SECONDS AWAY
In the year 2001 over 32 bottles of whisky were sold overseas each second (source: The Scotch Whisky Association).

Also: Exports

[Bold text within paragraphs refers to sub-headings in the Index]

SENIORITY

Whilst the Distillery Manager was clearly in charge, it was the wrath of the **Head Cooper** that any pilferers feared. The Cooper was very proud of his casks and, naturally, he was determined that their security was not compromised. It was not uncommon for a zealous Head Cooper to spend most of his daily shift checking his casks (source: Exciseman Anonymous).

Also: Willie's Leaker

SHAPES AND SIZES

Dalmore Distillery has a total of 8 stills; 2 large and 2 small wash stills and 2 large and 2 small spirit stills. But the most extraordinary thing that you will notice is that they have flat tops and the smaller spirit stills have straight-sided necks. As with so much in the **tradition** of the whisky industry, nobody is prepared to spell out the reason for this extraordinary configuration, not least because there is no written record of why on earth they were built like that in the first place.

The author favoured the practical explanation (applicable to much of the installation of equipment over the years at numerous distilleries): the roof was too low for the more conventional **shape of still** and so they decided to 'lop a bit off'. The straight-sided neck of the spirit stills, encased in a unique **water jacket** which acts as a cooling mechanism for the still, is another matter. As the Distillery Manager pointed out to those on the tour, the straight sides make it difficult for the **heavier vapours** to climb up to the **lyne arm** and so it is only the lightest vapours which make it over the top, to then condense into the new make spirit. These heavier vapours are returned into the still during the **reflux process** to be re-distilled and then, if lightened sufficiently, will pass over and through the lyne arm to the condenser.

Little wonder that distillers tamper with the shape of their stills at their peril.

Also: Purifiers; Sweetness

SHERRY BUTTS

Those from Europe are most probably made from oak grown in **Northern Spain**, dried in the south and filled with sherry for varying lengths of time. After it has served its life as a sherry cask, it may be '**toasted**' and is then ready for whisky. Sherry butts have a long life span and can be used more than once (source: The Scotch Malt Whisky Society).

Also: Toasting; Wood Sourcing

SHETLAND ISLANDS

There are working distilleries on the islands of **Arran, Islay, Jura, Mull, Orkney** and **Skye**. Subject to successful fund-raising (now under way) Shetland will soon be able to add its name to this roll call when, according to the Share Prospectus issued by **Blackwood Distillers Holdings plc** 'The whisky brand will be available for sale from 2007'.

SHIPPING

The owner of **Craigellachie Distillery** in 1922 – one 'Restless Peter' – moved 2,300 casks of whisky from the distillery to warehouses in **Campbeltown** in order to benefit from the **maritime atmosphere** during maturation. Not only did the journey involve a fleet of trains to reach the port of Lossiemouth, where the casks were then transferred aboard two steamers, but the vessels then had to safely negotiate the hazardous passage around **Cape Wrath** and down the Atlantic seaboard to the **Mull of Kintyre** (source: John Dewar & Sons Ltd).

Also: Fog; Salmon

SIGN HERE!

Marketing the product is as competitive today as it was 100 years ago and the innovations dreamed up by the inspirational marketing teams are endless. That's how it must seem for the unfortunate Distillery Manager who has to sign his way through some 2,000 – 4,000 labels for the occasional **special**

[Bold text within paragraphs refers to sub-headings in the Index]

bottlings. The author's arrival at **Glenmorangie** provided a welcome rest!

Also: Niche Markets

SIMILARITIES
One of the two famous sons of **John Dewar**, Tommy, might have been thinking of the whiskies produced in Scotland's distilleries, when he remarked that 'No two people are alike and both of them are glad of it'.

Also: Dewarisms

SIMPLE STUPID
How refreshing to find talented minds in the industry turning their attention to the need to market a clearly understood product to potential whisky drinkers. The **Easy Drinking Whisky Company** cuts right to the chase and produces 'The Smooth Peaty One', 'The Rich Spicy One' and 'The Smokey Peaty One'. What could be more simple.

SINGLE GRAIN WHISKY
This is the product of one **Grain Whisky distillery** (source: The Scotch Whisky Association).

Also: Grain Whisky

SINGLE MALT WHISKY
This is the product of one **Malt Whisky distillery** (source: The Scotch Whisky Association).

Also: Vatted Malt; Blended Scotch Whisky

SISKIN
A member of the finch family, this small bird is the symbol of Royal Brackla Distillery (source: John Dewar & Sons Ltd).

SLOW
The Distillery owner, accustomed to driving fast sports cars, sped in to the Distillery yard only to be confronted with a large

Clydesdale pulling a heavy cart loaded with newly filled casks. Standing on the brakes and swerving, collision was avoided. Horse and driver were unperturbed, but the Proprietor was furious. Storming into the office and having assembled the Manager, Brewer and Office Staff, he declared that the **Carter and Horse** had to go. Twenty minutes later all was forgiven and in time, a 15 mph sign was erected at the entrance to the Distillery (source: Exciseman Anonymous).

SMELL AND TASTE

As if the **Master Blender's** task was not difficult enough as it stands, his reluctance to resort to tasting can hide some astonishing surprises – as the author discovered. Some maturing whisky can smell sweet – 'just like honey' – but this can mask an astonishingly **bitter taste** (source: distillery visit).

Also: Blender's Nose

SNIFTER

Contrary to expectations, not someone who has misplaced their handkerchief, but rather, the name given to a **balloon shaped glass** where the neck is narrower than the base, so allowing the drinker to nose and enjoy the bouquet and

[Bold text within paragraphs refers to sub-headings in the Index]

character of the dram. Also used in parts of Scotland in reply to the question 'are you for a dram'? 'Aye! just a snifter, please'.

Also: Anosmia

SOAP

There is a device on the wash still at **Glen Deveron** Distillery which permitted a portion of a bar of white soap to be screwed down and cut off, allowing the soap to fall into the still. This inhibited excessive **frothing** in the still, a system now replaced by the addition of **anti-surfactant** liquid soaps (source: John Dewar & Sons Ltd).

Also: Macduff Distillery

SOUR BEER

Better known as **wash** this is the alcoholic liquid derived in turn from the **fermentation** of the liquid from the **mashing** process. Fermentation is induced in vessels called **wash backs** by the introduction of distillers' **yeast.** Such is the fermentation activity, that expansion space in the wash backs usually allows for a 33 per cent increase in volume. Unlike in **brewing**, all of the yeast is fermented out of the wash (source: from 'The Grain To The Glass' by J. & G. Grant).

Also: Aberlour Distillery

SPAIN

Two thirds of Scotch consumed in this country is downed in bars between midnight and four in the morning! (source: The Independent Spirit, December, 2002).

SPEY ROYAL

The young student, helping the local barman (who laboured under a speech defect), was asked to fetch a case of 'spare oil'. On double-checking why on earth he wanted this, the barman retorted 'for drinking'. Fortunately, the penny dropped and the Spey Royal was duly re-stocked (source: V. Cantlay, Torphins).

Also: Pronunciation

SPILE THE KNOT

If you are fortunate enough to visit a distillery where the **wash backs** are made from the traditional **Douglas Fir (Oregon Pine)**, check to see if the vat builder has used the modern threaded steel rods to 'hoop' the vat, as at **Balblair Distillery**. The vat builder's art is now confined to only one or two firms in Scotland and one of the foremost is that of **Joseph Brown** in **Dufftown**. The massive staves are butted with no seal between them. Using the modern, solid, round steel bars as 'hoops' cuts down on the need for manpower to tap the traditional thin flat metal hoops into place. Four men can now undertake a task which previously would have required, perhaps, double the number. The end of the metal rod is threaded and, by means of a device similar to the mechanism used to tighten a hose clip on the garden tap, the massive circular steel rod is tightened up to encircle the new vat in its grip.

An anxious wait of some seven days then ensues (for any distillery manager in a rush to re-start production) because the vat requires to be soaked in water to swell the wood and test for any leaks. The **vat builder** has already selected quality timber with minimal **knots** (known weak points) but inevitably the inside pressure from the water will seek out any weak points. The 'vat boys' will then return, bore out the offending weak point(s) and 'spile the knot' by driving in a wooden plug, or 'spile'.

Also: Fermentation; Important Stages; Hands On

SPRINGBANK DISTILLERY

If a distillery could possibly be described as enchanting then it must surely be here at the long established family business of J. and A. Mitchell. As **Aultmore** is to automation, so Springbank is to **tradition**. It's a long haul to reach **Campbeltown**, but worth every moment. For those with more than a passing interest in 'the cratur', ring in advance for an appointment and make the effort: soon (source: distillery visit).

Also: Adaptability; Contrasting Longevity; Cycle Of Production;

[Bold text within paragraphs refers to sub-headings in the Index]

Distillation: Times 2.5; Equality Of The Sexes; Foggy Nights;
Glengyle; Good Neighbours; Grist To The Mill; Hard Work;
Lime; Metric or Imperial; Production Process

SPRING WATER

Bruichladdich Distillery currently uses the spring water from **Octomore Farm** to reduce the percentage alcohol strength of their matured whisky in readiness for bottling. Bruichladdich intend to bottle **Islay Spring Water** as a separate commodity so that connoisseurs may enhance their dram (should they so wish) in the comfort of their own fireside (source: distillery visit).

Also: Octomore; Water

SS POLITICIAN

Compton Mackenzie and his legendary 'Whisky Galore' was perhaps thinking of other unfortunate vessels. For example, the 'Charlemagne' sailing from Greenock on her maiden voyage – with a cargo which included numerous whisky barrels – and which foundered off **Feochaig** in Kintyre. Although not commemorated in literary circles, the **Ballad of The Charlemagne** (sung to the tune of 'Hey Johnnie Cope') was committed to verse, to remember the heroic exploits of one Allan McLean and other locals, in their rescue of the crew and Captain – not to mention the cargo (source: The Kintyre Antiquarian and Natural History Society Magazine, Number Four, 1978).

Also: Nancy Whiskey

STACK 'EM HIGH

The traditional **dunnage warehouse**, with its earthen floor and stone walls (as seen for example at **Balblair Distillery**), has sufficient space to stack the maturing barrels three-high. By contrast, modern warehouses – for example the extensive complex at **Mulben** (west of Keith) – stack seven-nine-twelve high. Many modern warehouses have walls made from corrugated cladding sheets. It has been pointed out to the author that with the air at the top of the multiple stacks being drier, there will inevitably be differences within the same batch of maturing whisky according to which level is sampled (distillery visits).

Also: Distillery Mould; Pallets

STAINLESS STEEL
Despite the undeniable and it has to be said, not fully understood, properties of copper which are beneficial to the manufacturing process, stainless steel has certain uses within the industry. It is a much more durable metal than copper. Consequently, the copper **steam heating coils** (inside the stills) which are very susceptible to the **corrosive effects** of the boiling liquids are increasingly being replaced with stainless steel. This has resulted in satisfactory economies without any detrimental effect to the end product (source: Forsyths Group, Rothes).

Also: Copper; Lauter Tun

Author's note: stainless steel is now widely used in the manufacture of the **mash tun** (for soaking the **malted barley**) and the **wash backs** (for the fermentation process). There remain some distilleries, however, which continue to replace old timber with new timber.

STAVES
Unlike ships' planks which were traditionally bent into shape by the application of steam and pressure, the staves used in the manufacture of whisky barrels initially derive their shape from the process known as **charring**. The fact that this charring also serves to draw out the unpleasant sulphurs from the maturing whisky is an unquestionable bonus.

Also: Charring

STEP 4
'Contemplate it, savour it, but never rush it ....': extract from advice given on how to drink a certain malt (source: 'Really Taste Laphroaig' – a leaflet from the said distillery).

[Bold text within paragraphs refers to sub-headings in the Index]

STILL A RESTAURANT

Having already built a mini-brewery at his restaurant complex, a **Finnish restaurateur** commissioned two copper stills to establish a 'distillery' on site (using the mash from his mini-brewery). With a capacity of 350 litres from the spirit still, this should be adequate for an 'aperitif' and a 'digestif' (source: Forsyths Group, Rothes).

Also: Cornwall

STILL LIFE

The average **life-span** of certain areas of the **copper still** is about 10 – 12 years, but some parts will last as long as 25 – 30 years (source: Forsyths Group, Rothes). However to prove the exception to the rule, at **Tomintoul Distillery** they estimate a five year life for the base of the oil-fired steam heated stills and the upper portion of the still, some seven years

Also: Copper (the metal); Wear and Tear

STORAGE CAPACITY

One unforeseen consequence of the large industrial **Maltings** becoming the prime source of **malted barley** for nearly all of the distilleries is that a few distilleries are still in possession of considerable malt storage facilities. Thus **Balmenach** which uses 100 tonnes per week, but which used to be a supplier of malt from its own maltings plant to other distilleries, has perfect storage hoppers for some 2,500 tonnes. Distilleries such as this can therefore buy up any left over malted barley from the previous season at an attractive price. **Glen Moray** is another with excess storage space in their **malt bins** and here they use the excess capacity to allow the malt to further mature, which in turn benefits the subsequent stages of production (source: distillery visits).

Also: Maltings

SULPHIDES

Anecdotal evidence points to the fact that distillery drinking by employees was seldom from the maturing casks in the first three years. The old hands had learned to be patient and wait until the worst of the sulphurous impurities in the new make spirit had been leached out by the **charring** of the inner surface of the barrels (source: distillery visits).

Also: Pecking Order; Salad Cream

SUPERMARKET INFLUENCE

Distillers supplying certain of the supermarket chains are required to produce evidence which demonstrates that the malted barley which they are using has not originated from a **G.M. crop**. Similarly, driven by fear of inappropriate publicity and adverse **consumer reaction**, supermarkets may demand to see the **waste treatment processes** adhered to by the distilleries whose products are displayed on their shelves, especially if these are '**own brand**' labels. The traditional **blending trough** with its seemingly unhygienic conditions is also a 'no no' for the (adverse) publicity-sensitive supermarkets (source: distillery visits).

Also: Blended Scotch Whisky; Waste Not Want Not

SWEETNESS

During the distillation process, it is the **lighter alcohols** that help to generate this expression on the palate. The tall still necks at **Glenmorangie** and at **Tomintoul** distilleries are ideal in this respect – only the lightest of the alcohols can climb all the way up to the **lyne arm** and run down into the condenser. By contrast at **Ardbeg**, a broadly similar result from much **shorter stills** is achieved with the introduction of a **purifier pipe**. This draws off the **heavier alcohols** and feeds these back down into the bottom of the still, from whence they are re-cycled during the distillation process (source: distillery visits).

Also: Purifiers; Shapes and Sizes

SWIMMING POOL

In the town of **Bowmore** on Islay, the village swimming pool

[Bold text within paragraphs refers to sub-headings in the Index]

is located in an old distillery warehouse adjacent to Bowmore Distillery and the water is heated by the **waste hot water** from the distillation process (source: distillery visit).

Also: Eels

T

TAMNAVULIN DISTILLERY

This distillery, currently owned by **Whyte & Mackay,** is located in the tiny village of **Tomnavoulin** on the banks of the **River Livet** and bears out the fact that Gaelic was once a language of these parts (as in 'Toman a' Mhuilinn' or little knoll of the mill (source: History of the Celtic Place Names of Scotland, W.J. Watson 1926).

Author's note: c.f. **Lag a' Mhuilinn** on Islay (the mill in the hollow).

TANKED-UP

Inventors should note that their skills could potentially lead to an early and comfortable retirement, if they can devise a fool-proof method which shows that the volume of **alcohol** pumped into the **road tanker** equates with the volume pumped out at its subsequent destination. The author has been assured by 'those in the know' that, despite every endeavour and due to factors such as temperature change; tyre pressure variation; idiosyncrasies of gauged vessels; spillages and 'other causes', comparison of the two figures rarely tallies (source: Exciseman Anonymous).

Also: Whisky and Ice

TASTING (LONG DISTANCE)

When the Scotch Malt Whisky Society organised its first tasting in **Sydney** in 2002, some of those attending had flown specifically from **Perth** in Western Australia – equivalent to nipping over from **Istanbul** for a dram in '**The Vaults**' at their Edinburgh headquarters (source: The Scotch Malt Whisky Society Newsletter spring 2003).

[Bold text within paragraphs refers to sub-headings in the Index]

TAX

In the United Kingdom, 70 per cent of the **retail price** of a typical bottle of standard blended Scotch Whisky is accounted for by tax (source: The Scotch Whisky Association).

Also: Revenue Value

TAXATION

Landmark dates include: 1644 when the **Scots' Parliament** introduced a tax on '**aquavitae** or other strong liquor'; 1823 when a British Parliamentary Act sanctioned **legal distilling** and imposed a formula for licensing and taxation; 1995, when, for the first time in one hundred years, the British government reduced the level of taxation on whisky (source: The Scotch Whisky Association).

TESTING

Long before automation was introduced, bottling was being conducted by hand in a warehouse where the Manager retrieved a bottle from the bottling line to check the strength of the spirit. The sample was taken to the office shared with the Excise and duly poured into a sample jar for testing. The Manager was distracted by a phone call, and the **Excise Officer** present swapped the sample with a jar of over-proof spirit taken from a vat which was to be reduced in strength. The Manager proceeded to test his sample: consternation! The instrument indicated that the spirit was above bottling strength and probably over-proof. This suggested that bottling was in progress from the wrong vat. The poor man rushed from the Office shouting "Stop! Stop!" and the **bottling line** ground to a halt. However, all was well and the Officer confirmed the swap of samples to a much relieved Manager. A few drams later and the incident was enjoyed and forgotten (source: Exciseman Anonymous).

Also: Bouncing Bottles; Water Test

THREE INTO TWO

Never known to pass up the opportunity to save money, a

canny cooper had observed that, if he took the **staves** from the **sheaves** of three imported **bourbon barrels**, he could make two **dump hogsheads**. The result of his astute eye was that warehouses could now stock significantly more whisky in less space (source: Dennis Malcolm, Balmenach).

Also: Capacities

THREE SHEETS IN THE WIND*

Steady as she goes! – as some 100 yachts now participate in the annual (July) **Classic Malts Cruise** fourteen days out from Oban. Started in 1994, this thoroughly relaxing itinerary only requires crew to check-in to the **Diageo** distilleries at **Oban**, **Talisker** and **Lagavulin** on specific dates for pre-arranged ceilidhs and hospitality. For seasoned hands there is time to visit other island haunts on **Mull**, **Jura** and of course Islay itself. It's a breeze!

* The origin of the expression stems from a sailing ship going 'head to wind'. This results in its sails flapping around uncontrollably: just like an inebriated person staggers around.

TIDES

Some of the warehouses at **Bowmore** Distillery, where the whisky casks lie maturing, are built so close to the sea that when the tide comes in the seaward wall can be lapped by water (source: distillery visit).

Also: Swimming Pool

TIRING WORK

A Speyside 'Bobby', in the days of patrol by bicycle to the local distillery, always made a point of visiting the Manager, Brewer and Cooper. Each proved equally hospitable. On one occasion, and in the absence of management, the Policeman was subsequently heard to remark 'That the young Excise was gie thochtless just offering ae dram' (source: Exciseman Anonymous).

Also: Crossed Wires; Dramming; Pecking Order

[Bold text within paragraphs refers to sub-headings in the Index]

TOASTING

The oak **staves** from which whisky barrels are made, were originally softened over a small fire in order to bend them into the requisite curved shape. Nowadays, **cooperages** soften the wood with steam. However, the insides of the barrels continue to be toasted by the coopers (nowadays using infra-red technology) because it has been established for quite some time that treating the new wood in this manner has a beneficial effect on the end product. Toasting breaks down the wood's **hemicellulose** (a complex carbohydrate) into simple **sugars**. These then caramelise in the heat, and this caramelised sugar adds both flavour and colour to the whisky. **Lignins** also are affected by the toasting. These break down into **phenols**, which can lend a smoky flavour to whisky, and into **vanillin**, a **phenolic aldehyde** that supplies a whiff of **vanilla** to the spirit. 'Charring' is a quite different process from toasting and the resultant charcoal coating to the inside of the barrel serves to remove some of the harsher sulphurous characteristics of the new make spirit – in addition to performing many of the functions associated with toasting.

Also: Charring; Pompeying

TODDY

Although often associated with a handy cure for the **common cold**, being a mixture of a sweetened hot water and whisky, the Oxford Dictionary notes that it is 'The fresh or fermented sap of various species of **palm**, used as beverage'.

Also: Measles

TOMATIN DISTILLERY

This titan of a distillery (owned by the Japanese company '**Takara-Shuzo-Marubeni**') has reduced its production capacity from the 23 stills in the late 1970's to the present 12 stills, with respective maximum output of 11 million and 5 million litres of alcohol per annum (source: distillery visit).

Also: Eels

TONNES AND LITRES

Visitors to distilleries often like to hear some useful facts and figures. One American, on a very personal tour with the author at **Glenfarclas**, just would not give up! Here 16.5 tonnes of **malted barley** are producing approximately 10,000 litres of **new make spirit** ready for maturation in casks. This equates to approximately one tonne of barley per 600 litres of new make spirit. But, given that, in a ten year period, there will be an approximate annual 2 per cent evaporation loss, the possible volume for bottling reduces to some 480 litres. It follows that a tonne of barley might produce approximately 686 bottles (70cl) of Glenfarclas. We all parted with a huge sigh of relief, the astute citizen remarking that the 95,000 litres of water used in each production batch was working out at roughly 138 litres per bottle of whisky: a figure which does not include the water used for cooling and other industrial processes, such as cleaning.

Also: Metric Or Imperial; Water

TRADITION

Much is made of this as a **marketing concept** by the whisky industry. Specific companies pursue this to varying degrees and a number of distillers now specifically carry this through to production. At **Balmenach** they proudly state that 'It is company policy to keep tradition'. **Springbank** clearly revels in the old and trusted, and **Bruichladdich** has left few in any doubt as to the value which they place upon the practical implementation of tradition in the manufacturing process.

In the course of the research for this book, the author formed the opinion that with the concentration of operating distilleries into fewer and larger ownership groupings (and their inevitable desire to maximise profitability) there must increasingly be a place in the industry for those with the unique product that only the traditional equipment and processes can manufacture.

Also: Ownership

[Bold text within paragraphs refers to sub-headings in the Index]

TRAINS AND BOATS AND PLANES

'What's in the packaging?' you may ask. The answer includes The Macallan **Travel Range** of 50cl bottles in their most attractive containers, depicting **Atlantic Liners, Steam Trains** and **Flying Boats**. Check it out! (source: distillery visit).

Also: Empress of Australia; Queen Mary 2

TRANSPORT

As reported in 'Scotland On Sunday' (June, 2003) the largest owner of Scottish distilleries transports 65 per cent of its Scottish-produced drink by sea, 30 per cent by rail and 5 per cent by road. Whilst not indicative of the whisky industry as a whole (it includes drinks other than whisky from grain distilleries), it nevertheless demonstrates the significance of **sea transport**.

Also: Ballindalloch

TUBE

The tube-like carton in which many whisky bottles nowadays are sold was first introduced by **Wm Grant & Sons** to help launch their **Glenfiddich** brand in the late 1960s.

Also: Plastic

TUNNEL VISION

The whisky smugglers along the **Kintyre Peninsula** had an eye for terrain when they made full use of the tunnel which ran up from the sea near **Rosehill Farm**. Archibald Armour of Rosehill (1850 – 1918) was the last to walk through the tunnel before it was closed off, due to danger of collapse (source: Miss Flora Petrie, Kippen and great grand-daughter to A. Armour).

Also: Glenbucket

U

USHER HALL

Funds for the construction of this fine concert hall in Edinburgh came from **Andrew Usher**, one of the businessmen who rebuilt **Royal Brackla** Distillery in the late 19th century (source: John Dewar & Sons Ltd).

Also: Glenlivet

V

VANISHING DISTILLERIES
Some names to conjure with:
Cairnarget, Caul, Corn Cairn, Lesmurdie, Manbeen, New Seat.

VAT BUILDER
The massive vats used in the old traditional wooden **wash backs** (to ferment the **mash**) require quite separate construction skills from those of the cooper working with casks. The most obvious difference is being able to deal with the sheer size. Another lies in understanding the different pressures which exist, especially in the case of the wash backs. Here the **fermentation** can be so vigorous that the side walls 'move' (source: distillery visits).

Also: Fermentation; Spile The Knot

VAT 69
William Sanderson invited some of his friends to his offices in Leith in 1882 to sample a number of blended whiskies. The preference was for the one in vat number 69 and so a brand was born.

Also: Brand Protection

VATTED MALT
The Scotch Whisky Association, 2002 publication 'Scotch Whisky Questions and Answers' explains that combining malt whisky with malt whisky (or, grain whisky with grain whisky) is known as **vatting** and gives rise to the term vatted malt as depicted on some whisky bottle labels. Intriguingly, some blenders maintain that it is much more difficult to produce a good vatted malt, than it is to produce a good blended whisky.

This is because of the key role that grain whisky plays in harmonising and pulling together the individual flavours of the constituent malts in a blended whisky. A vatted malt can contain many different malts, but it will NOT contain any grain whiskies. For example, **Chivas Century** is a vatting of 100 malts (source: Charles MacLean in The Scotch Malt Whisky Society Newsletter spring 2003).

Also: Pure Malt

VICE CONSUL

An early owner of **Bowmore** Distillery – James Mutter – was the Ottoman, Portuguese and Brazilian Vice-Consul in Glasgow. His far-flung connections helped the Bowmore name to become established in the 19th century.

Also: Bowmore

VISITOR CENTRES

The first purpose-built Visitor Centre was opened by **Wm. Grant & Sons** at **Glenfiddich Distillery** in 1969 and, as with so much that this pioneering company has done, others have followed. Some distillers would probably admit that they are not demonstrably cost effective. On the other hand, their value as an effective form of marketing cannot be overlooked. In addition, some such premises have been designed with corporate visitors in mind, so generating added value from the initial outlay.

Those distilleries which are organised to receive copious numbers of visitors have found it essential to adhere to a very regimented **tour**. The upshot is a maximum of 40 minutes with the Guide, followed by an opportunity to pursue more detailed questions at the end of the tour – dram in hand. Unfortunately, other than for the more dogged of inquisitors, this can result in much being glossed over.

How long one will be able to continue to visit distilleries that are not additionally staffed to cope with the inquisitive public is a matter of conjecture.

Also: Distillery Visits

[Bold text within paragraphs refers to sub-headings in the Index]

VISITORS

To this day, and despite the best efforts of The **Health & Safety Executive** and the litigious times we live in, many distilleries which do not have purpose-built Visitor Centres continue to make every endeavour to show genuinely interested members of the public around 'the works'. There can be few industries elsewhere in the country which are so accommodating. It is an attitude that perhaps reflects the **farming roots** of the industry and, certainly, the pride of the workforce.

W

WAIT FOR WEIGHT

Little wonder that the traditional **dunnage warehouse** rarely saw the maturing whisky racked higher than three levels. Until suitable hoists were introduced, the movement of a full **barrel**, **hogshead**, or **butt**,* weighing in at 203 kilos, 254 kilos and 508 kilos required as much skill as strength

Also: Pallets

* 200, 250, 500 litres respectively.

WAREHOUSE TEMPERATURE

A traditional **dunnage warehouse** retains a constant temperature throughout the year of 8 – 9 degrees Celsius and, with casks stacked only 2 or 3 high, there is very little difference in temperature within the warehouse. By contrast some modern warehouses (such as those at **The Macallan**) will stack upwards of 9 high and **temperature** and **humidity** within the warehouse is carefully controlled. There are, however, modern warehouses which do not have **air conditioning**.

Also: Dunnage Warehouses; Experiments

WAREHOUSING

Some distilleries, for example **The Macallan**, will store their maturing whisky so that different years' production is mixed throughout the warehouse(s). This ensures that should there be any serious accident, the complete batch is not lost. Whereas a company that is bottling a single malt will be anxious to ensure that there is no significant difference between casks (especially from those stored in multiple racks in modern warehouses), the **Blender** can afford to take a slightly more relaxed approach, in the knowledge that he has the expertise to off-set any slight variations that may exist.

Also: Indispensable; Pallets

WARRANTS

The only distilleries today to hold the **Royal Warrant** designation are **Knockando** and **Laphroaig**. Blenders having gained this accolade are **Johnnie Walker & Sons; John Dewar & Sons; William Sanderson & Sons** (VAT 69); **Berry Bros. & Rudd** (Cutty Sark); **Hill Thomson & Co** (Queen Anne) and **Matthew Gloag & Sons** (The Famous Grouse) (source: Charles MacLean in The Scotch Malt Whisky Society's issue 97 May, 2002).

WASTE NOT, WANT NOT

The industry prides itself in striving to ensure that nothing is wasted in the production of whisky. At **Springbank**, even the '**coomings**'* from the mill are gathered and eventually added to the **mash** (source: distillery visit).

* see Chambers Scots Dictionary: 'coom – the dust of grain' and so the term used at Springbank for the roots which are removed from the malted barley, before it is passed through the mill.

Also: Grist To The Mill; Supermarket Influence

WASTE TREATMENT

Much has changed since the days when the **North East River Purification Board** granted approvals for the dumping of distillery waste into the North Sea. Lorries loaded with **Pot Ale** and **Spent Lees** were a regular feature a-top the Moray Firth sea cliffs near **Portnockie** (one of a number of approved locations). As a young Planning Officer in the early 1970's, the author would watch as the tanker's hose was placed over the cliff edge and the waste liquid dumped.

Today, **The Scottish Environment Protection Agency** (**SEPA**) (which superseded these regional authorities) insists that waste liquids are pumped out through a long out-fall pipe, where the currents will rapidly disperse the effluent (for example near **Port Askaig** on The **Sound of Islay**). The stricter legislation has encouraged the whisky industry to process for resale as much of its waste as possible. The most common by-product is animal feed: **Dark Grains**.

Approximately half of Scotland's malt distilleries send their **Draff** and **Pot Ale** to specialist **Dark Grains Plants** where the waste is transformed into nutritious **animal feed**. Volumes of waste from individual distilleries are relatively small and there are a sufficient number of plants to handle the waste from the numerous malt whisky distilleries.

However, the **Grain Distilleries** with their vastly greater levels of production often have their own Dark Grains Plant on site, because of economies of scale. This has the adverse effect, however, of making the grain distillery heavily dependent upon the efficiency of its **waste treatment plant**. For example, at **Invergordon Grain Distillery**, if the highly complicated Dark Grains Plant should falter and be unable to continue processing the waste from the distillery, then within 4-5 hours the complete distillery has to cease production (source: distillery visit).

Also: Coastal Effluent; Control Of Pollution Act; Government Regulations

WATCHER

This delightful title summed up the role of the Excise Officer's **Revenue Assistant**. His duties were quite simply to ensure the workers left empty-handed and that lorries were correctly loaded/unloaded. There was usually one watcher per warehouse door. The Watcher held the '**crown lock keys**' during working hours and at other times these were kept secure in the '**revenue box**' in the **excise office** at each distillery. The Government introduced a major change to excise supervision at traders' premises in 1983 and by 1987 the last of the Watchers had been dispensed with.

Also: Customs & Excise

WATER

Vast quantities of water go into making whisky. At a conference dealing with Scotland's Mountains and Water in the 21st Century, held in Perth on 20 – 21 January, 2003, it

[Bold text within paragraphs refers to sub-headings in the Index]

was stated that it requires approximately 4 litres of water to produce 1 litre of whisky. Evidence given by The Malt Distillers' Association to the Scottish Parliament in September 2002 illustrated how, in the context of the **River Spey Catchment**, the Malt Whisky Distilling Industry abstracted 1.81 million cubic metres per annum for Mashing and borrowed 27.15 million cubic metres* for cooling purposes. Despite the fact that most cooling water is returned to the watercourse from whence it has been abstracted, it is little wonder that distilleries covet their own source of water, especially for the mashing process.

Also: Control of Pollution Act; Feuds

* I cubic metre = 1,000 litres

WATER TEST

The traditional method to test the quality of the **new make spirit** is to add water. If the resultant mixture remains crystal clear it is top quality; if it turns cloudy then it is **inferior spirit**.

Also: Testing

WEAR AND TEAR

Distilleries are theatres of incessant activity and moving parts. The **copper stills** give the impression of sedate and grand statues, but they too eventually require replacing. Using modern electronic measuring techniques, specific parts of the new 6mm thick copper stills will be repaired or replaced when the copper has been worn down to 2mm (source: distillery visit).

Also: Still Life

WELDING

Rivets, bolts and welding are the methods used by the coppersmiths to join the sheets of copper, in order to make the gentle curves of the copper stills. You can spot innumerable variations as you go around the distilleries, but they all have one thing in common, they require to be foolproof.

Consequently, **Dalmore's** claim to have one of the oldest welded joints in operation is not to be taken lightly. This is doubly true when you see the unique castellated join of the two panels. Here, brass filings were used by the welders in 1874 as the binding molten metal.

Also: Riveted

WHAT'S IN A NAME?

When it comes to the subject under discussion perhaps, not surprisingly, it is **glen**. By far the most popular **prefix** for Scotch Whisky is this Scottish term for a narrow valley – as in Glen Sloy. The Scotch Whisky Association lists the *principal brands* of its constituent members and the next most popular prefix (excluding extensions of the one brand) is **old** – as in Old Mull – with half as many entries.

Also: Blends Blends Blends; Glenbucket

WHAT'S YOURS?

The young businessman from Northern Ireland was staying a night in the Aberlour Hotel in Speyside. This being his first incursion into the North East of Scotland, he was not yet acquainted with the need to adapt to the **local dialect**. Whilst awaiting the hour for evening dinner, he went into the Bar and greeted the solitary old character leaning on the bar, with his customary address from home: 'How are you doing?' 'I'll hae a nip', he replied (source: Exciseman Anonymous).

Is it a Bruichladdich* you'll be havin'?
Or perhaps a neat Bunnahabhain?
I'll have a Dalmore,
And a dram of Tormore
Then your soft cosy bed I'll be havin'.

* Also: Pronunciation

WHEAT

Most Scotch Whisky drinkers who know a little about the product they are drinking, will be aware that **barley** is the grain

[Bold text within paragraphs refers to sub-headings in the Index]

most commonly associated with their dram. The numerous traditional distilleries producing their single malts use only (malted) barley. It may therefore come as something of a surprise to know that almost as much wheat is used by the **Scotch Whisky Industry**. This is because the seven **grain distilleries** in Scotland use the most economical grain that will meet their specification. The bulk of this is supplied by Scottish farmers (for example, some 80 per cent of the wheat used by **Invergordon Grain Distillery** comes from farms north of The Central Belt). Specialist companies such as **Scotgrain Agriculture Ltd** buy in the vast quantities required and sell this on to the grain distillers. The wholesalers monitor standards and, in conjunction with the Whisky Industry, undertake scientific trials (just as is done with barley) to ensure that the crop is of the very highest standard and meets the demands of the industry.

It should be noted that the grain distillers have to use some barley because the barley contains the **diastase** necessary to convert the **starch** in the wheat (or other grain) into **sugar**. Furthermore, a typical grain distillery will always avoid over-dependency on one supplier and one type of grain. **Maize** is the most likely alternative to wheat for the Scottish grain distilleries. As with so much in the Scotch Whisky Industry, price in relation to quality is the determining factor in deciding the volume of grain derived from any one type or source (distillery visits).

Also: Quantities of Grain

WHISKEY

Irish and American whiskey is differentiated by this spelling. However, two **American brands** follow the spelling convention adopted by the Scots, Canadians and the Japanese. The two exceptions are – **Makers Mark** and **Dickel** (source: Charles MacLean in The Scotch Malt Whisky Society Newsletter winter 2002).

Also: Bourbon Whiskey

WHISKY

Is a distilled spirit drink made from cereals, water and yeast – or, as one Head Brewer remarked: 'Whisky is essentially **distilled beer**.'

Also: Scots or Scotch?

WHISKY AND ICE

One winter's day the articulated lorry was returning to the station with a load of full barrels on a road which was very icy and rutted. Descending the steep **Delnashaugh** brae the lorry stubbornly refused to stay on the road and hit the parapet of the bridge, leaving the tractor unit hanging over a seven metre drop to the **River Avon** below. The driver gingerly inched across to the passenger door and stepped down into streams of whisky running along the icy ruts (source: Bill Murray, Fair Isle and formerly employed at Ballindalloch Station).

WHISKY ON WATER

For your next **party trick**, make the claim that you can drink pure water or pure whisky from the one glass that contains only these two liquids. 'Impossible,' say all your admiring party-goers – unless there is a scientist in the gathering. Fill the glass three-quarters full with water. Place a cloth (quality handkerchief or drying cloth is ideal) over the glass. With your fingers gently push the surface of the cloth down until it just makes contact with the water. Reach for the bottle of whisky and now pour gently onto the top of the cloth until the glass has been topped up with whisky. Now slide off the cloth cover, ask someone to pass you a straw and then proceed to drink either the neat whisky (the top layer) or the neat water (beneath the top layer). Alcohol is of course lighter than water (source: Drew Sinclair, Distillery Manager, Dalmore).

Also: Crossed Wires

WHITE HORSE

This blended whisky has its 'spiritual home' at **Lagavulin**

Distillery on Islay (source: The Islay and Jura Whisky Trail Leaflet). This particular brand of blended whisky serves to demonstrate the inter-dependence between competing companies in the industry. Lagavulin is owned by **Diageo**, but **Craigellachie** Distillery (The White Horse Distillery) is owned by **Bacardi** (John Dewar & Sons). The anomaly has its origins in the early 20th century when both distilleries were owned by the same company, Mackie & Co (Distillers) Ltd. The latter owned the White Horse brand of blended Scotch.

Also: Craigellachie; Horse Sense; Ownership

WHITE WHISKY

Spotted on the shelves of Duty Free, Malta Airport: TKO pure white Scotch Whisky, distilled, matured and bottled in Scotland by Burn Stewart Distillers, Glasgow, Scotland.

Also: New Make Spirit

WILLIE'S LEAKER

A bonding of newly filled casks was taking place under the watchful eyes of the Distillery owner and the young Excise Officer, when the owner remarked 'I think Willie has a leaker' – a reference to the '**Lea & Perrins**' bottle which was in the ruler-pocket of Willie's overalls. A visit to a **warehouse** was an opportunity not to be missed, and Willie was taking full advantage. Such were the relaxed attitudes, that neither the owner nor the Exciseman passed any further comment. The **Cooper** would have been more upset than anyone, but he didn't notice the incident and wasn't told. (source: Exciseman Anonymous).

Also: Salad Cream; Seniority

WINE

Fortunately for the dedicated staff at **Glenmorangie**, when opposition to their novel approach to developing new products was first raised by others in the industry, they were able to point out that the practice is centuries old. At that time, casks were so expensive that those arriving in Scotland full of **port, sherry, brandy** – or other wines and spirits – would be emptied out and refilled to dispatch **malt whisky** to all corners of the world. During the long sea voyages, the contents would take on characteristics that reflected the previous use of the casks.

In the early 1990s, Glenmorangie decided to revive this practice from the distant past. The result is a selection of single malts that add new and intriguing nuances to the classic taste of Scotland's favourite malt.

The original stimulus for much of this endeavour can be laid at the door of the then Distillery Manager at Glenmorangie – a certain **Dr Bill Lumsden** – and the Chief Accountant. Both gentlemen enjoyed their wine and were interested in its possible qualities for their own industry. From this evolved the company's revolutionary **Sauternes; Côtes de Nuits** and **Hermitage** wine finishes.

These '**guest finishes**' as they are termed command a price which reflects not only the pedigree of the vineyards, but also the additional time and labour in perfecting a unique new product. The actual finishing time in the wine casks can vary from approximately 18 – 36 months depending on the progress of each individual cask.

Also: Glen Moray

WIN SOME, LOSE SOME

During the maturation period, the average loss in volume to evaporation (the so-called '**Angels' Share**') is approximately 2 per cent per annum. However, at the more exposed **island distilleries**, such as those on Islay, this figure falls to around 1.5 per cent per annum, due to the higher **moisture content** in the atmosphere. The down-side is that this wetter air serves to dilute the **alcohol content** in the barrel. Spare a thought, however, for those producing the Amrut Single Malt in Bangalore, India where the climate results in some 10 per cent loss per annum to evaporation. Indeed such is the loss to the atmosphere that they have to bottle after four

[Bold text within paragraphs refers to sub-headings in the Index]

years maturation, otherwise they risk having little left to drink!

Also: Angels' Share

WOOD SOURCING

There was a time when the whisky producers' attitude to **casks** and **barrels** could be summed up (for most, although by no means all) as – 'If it doesn't leak, fill it'. Much has changed in the last thirty years, driven in no small measure by the spectacular leap in popularity of **single malts**. Today, many of the leading producers realise that the handling and the quality of the wood is of critical influence in determining the end product. Brands such as **The Macallan** and **Glenmorangie** take this to heart and now exert considerable influence over certain forests in **Galicia** and **Missouri** (respectively) from whence they obtain the timber for their casks (source: distillery visits).

Also: Flavour; Oak; Ozark Mountains

WORLD WAR

During the 1914 – 1918 and the 1939 – 1945 World Wars, in order to conserve **stocks of barley**, distilling was eventually reduced to a standstill by 1918 and 1944 respectively.

Also: Rationing

WORMS (TECHNICAL)

Ninety metres of coiled **copper tube** is what you will find inside the traditional condenser tub. Taking up considerably more space than the modern **shell and tube condensers** they might seem an easy candidate for modernisation, but those distilleries which have retained them – for example **Balmenach** – are adamant: there is no better alternative. Indeed there are two known incidents of distilleries reverting to the traditional worm after their attempts at modernisation failed to produce the quality of old.

Also: Moby Dick

WORMS (TEMPERANCE)

Mr H. Garrick of Kilmarnock recalls the annual visit of the local **Temperance Officer** to the school in the 1930s, warning the pupils about the **pitfalls of alcohol**. Producing a worm he would drop it into a small glass of whisky, whereupon it shrivelled up and died. Asking the class what lessons they had learned from this demonstration, one boy put his hand up and said 'Please Sir, if you drink plenty whisky you'll no' be bothered wi' worms'.

[Bold text within paragraphs refers to sub-headings in the Index]

X

XMAS

Christmas this year will be risky
As I fear my old Pa may get frisky
As he celebrates Yule,
With that high-octane fuel
The Society's Old Mortlach Whisky!

(Source: with kind permission of Alastair Singleton and The Wine
Society, Stevenage)

Y

YEAST
Distillers' yeast is the preferred type used for the fermentation process. This type of yeast ferments the malt sugars more thoroughly than **brewers' yeast** on its own. Some distilleries use a mix of both types of yeast claiming that this induces certain extra properties in the fermented wash – for example, a spicy aroma (source: R. Ryman, Head Brewer, St Austell Brewery).

Also: Important Stages

YIELD
Given that a number of the relatively remote distilleries located in the Inner Hebrides strive to obtain the maximum yield of **alcohol** per tonne of **malted barley**, it is ironic that some should use malted barley with such high **phenol contents**. The latter is known to result in a slightly lower yield of alcohol (source: distillery visit).

Also: Efficiency Measurement

[Bold text within paragraphs refers to sub-headings in the Index]

INDEX

Principal facts are in CAPITALS
Subsidiary facts are in lower case (separate entries are not included when a community, brand and distillery have the same name)

A

B

E

F

G

L

M

N

O

[Bold text within paragraphs refers to sub-headings in the Index]

S

U

V

W

X

Y